WORKPLACE LEARNING & PERFORMANCE ROLES

The
EVALUATOR

WILLIAM J. ROTHWELL

A Self-Guided Job Aid With Assessments Based on
ASTD Models for Workplace Learning and Performance

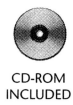

CD-ROM
INCLUDED

Linking People,
Learning & Performance

Ordering information: Books published by the American Society for Training & Development can be ordered by calling 800.628.2783 or 703.683.8100, or via the Website at www.astd.org.

Library of Congress Catalog Card Number: 00-100863

ISBN: 1-56286-139-5

TABLE OF CONTENTS

◢ LIST OF TABLES AND FIGURES

SECTION 1 GETTING STARTED

What Is the Background of This Project?

The Evaluator is an outgrowth of *ASTD Models for Workplace Learning and Performance* (Rothwell, Sanders, and Soper, 1999). It is a self-study job aid for the workplace learning and performance (WLP) practitioner that describes the competencies essential to success in the WLP field and contains information about the practitioner's role as evaluator. (Additional volumes in this ASTD series will focus on the practitioner's other roles. See ASTD's Website, www.astd.org, for information on these volumes as they are released.) Note that the term *role* here should not be confused with job title; rather, just as in theater the word *role* refers to the part that an actor plays, in WLP a role is a part that the practitioner plays in the human performance improvement (HPI) process. Following is a complete list of WLP roles (see also Rothwell et al., 1999, pages xv-xvii):

♦ The *manager* plans, organizes, schedules, and leads the work of individuals and groups to achieve desired results; facilitates the strategic plan; ensures that workplace learning and performance accord with organizational needs and plans; and ensures accomplishment of the administrative requirements of the function.

♦ The *analyst* isolates and troubleshoots the causes of "human performance gaps" and identifies areas in need of improvement.

♦ The *intervention selector* chooses appropriate learning and performance *interventions* (that is, corrective actions), both in and out of the workplace, to address the causes of these performance gaps.

♦ The *intervention designer and developer* formulates learning and performance interventions that address these causes and complement similarly targeted interventions.

♦ The *intervention implementor* ensures that the interventions that have been selected are carried out in an effective and appropriate way and complement similarly targeted interventions. In this capacity, the intervention implementor may serve as, for example, administrator, instructor, organization development practitioner, career development specialist, process redesign consultant, workspace designer, compensation specialist, or facilitator.

♦ The *change leader* inspires the workforce to embrace the interventions implemented, creates a direction for the effort, and ensures that the interventions are continually monitored and directed in ways that are consistent with stakeholders' desired results.

♦ The *evaluator* assesses the changes made, the actions taken, the results achieved, and the impact experienced and apprises participants and stakeholders accordingly.

What Does This Job Aid Contain, and How Do You Use It?

The Evaluator consists of both a book and an accompanying CD-ROM that is designed to enhance and test your knowledge. Read the written material first, and then use the CD-ROM to assess what you have learned. Practice using the worksheets and activities. For additional input, be sure to ask mentors or knowledgeable co-workers for one-on-one coaching.

Definitions

The WLP practitioner's role as evaluator is to assess the changes made from an intervention, the actions taken, the results achieved, and the impact experienced. The evaluator apprises participants and stakeholders about these matters, building on the work previously performed by the analyst. In short, it is the evaluator's task to determine how much and how well an intervention helped to solve a performance problem by closing the gap between actual and desired performance.

The evaluator's role can include, but is not limited to, training evaluation. *Training evaluation* examines the relative success of a training intervention. It may include examinations of how much participants liked the training, how much they learned from training, how much on-the-job behavior change resulted from training, and how much financial impact was realized by the organization from training (Kirkpatrick, 1994).

However, evaluators may also examine the impact of such nonlearning interventions as making improvements to recruitment, selection, job design, organizational design, reward and incentive systems, equipment and tools, and workplace design. Nonlearning evaluation examines the relative success of such interventions. It can focus on how much people liked the intervention, how much change occurred as a result of it, and how much impact the intervention has had on the organization (Rothwell, Hohne, and King, 2000).

In a sense, the evaluator's role focuses on *organizational performance evaluation*, which determines how well an organizational environment supports such important goals as improved performance, productivity, safety, and customer satisfaction, among other goals, and the interventions undertaken to realize those goals. The results of an organizational performance evaluation can be useful in improving the organization's performance and realizing the promise of a High-Performance Workplace (HPW).

Importance of the Evaluator's Role

No intervention can be evaluated until the facts and perceptions surrounding it are understood. Just as it is the analyst's role to uncover facts and perceptions surrounding performance problems and isolate

their cause(s), it is the evaluator's role to verify those facts and perceptions.

The evaluator's role is important because managers and other stakeholders of workplace learning and performance increasingly require evidence that investments of time, money, and other resources in intellectual capital development were worthwhile and exceeded their expense. (Intellectual capital development refers to any efforts made by an organization to increase the collective economic value of its workforce.) The evaluator's role is key because it ensures accountability by all participants involved in interventions—not just WLP professionals but also other stakeholders such as managers and workers. While many people may associate evaluation with after-the-fact assessments of results, the fact is that evaluation also should be carried out before and during interventions. Without evaluation, WLP professionals and others would not obtain sufficient feedback about the impact of their interventions to make continuous improvement efforts worthwhile— nor would they possess the information needed to demonstrate to critics that the interventions paid off.

The Relationship Between the Evaluator's Role and the Analyst's Role

The roles of evaluator and analyst are closely related and can be easily confused. For this reason, it is important to distinguish between them. While analysts identify performance problems and determine their causes, evaluators assess the results or impacts of interventions. In other words, analysts uncover *problems* and isolate their cause(s), while evaluators examine the *solutions* (interventions) and determine their results. Analysts and evaluators may pose similar questions, though their intentions may differ. Analysts want to find out what problems exist and what causes them. Evaluators want to find out whether interventions solved the problems, addressed the causes, and provided value-added benefits to the organization and its people.

Of course, there are occasions when the work of analyst and evaluator can be performed closely together. Although analysts typically perform their work before an intervention, these role distinctions can blur because evaluators can perform their work before, during, and after interventions. That can create some confusion—especially before an intervention when an analyst is interested in determining the cause of a problem while an evaluator might be interested in forecasting the benefits of a solution. Furthermore, it is possible that the same person may (or may not) be enacting both roles.

Both analysts and evaluators also share several competencies. For instance, both must apply the competency analytical thinking. But analysts apply that competency to problems and their consequences (effects), while evaluators apply it to solutions and their outcomes. Both analysts and evaluators also must apply the competency performance gap analysis, which compares actual and ideal performance levels. Here, analysts focus their attention on the differences before an intervention is undertaken, while evaluators may focus their attention on the differences before, during and after the intervention is undertaken. If the analyst has enacted his or her role successfully, evaluators should not need to repeat the work performed by them. (If that is not the case or if different people enact these roles, double-checking may be necessary.)

Unique to the evaluator's role are such competencies as analyzing performance data and intervention monitoring. By definition, analyzing performance data occurs after an intervention is undertaken and is intended to determine the intervention's effects. Intervention monitoring focuses attention on aligning the intervention with organizational strategies during implementation.

What Are Competencies, and Why Are They Important?

Competencies are characteristics that underlie successful performance: "internal capabilities that people bring to their jobs, capabilities which may be expressed in a broad, even infinite, array of on-the-job behaviors" (McLagan, 1989, page 77). Competencies have commanded growing attention because they distinguish the *exemplary* performers (best-in-class) from the *fully successful* (standard, but nothing more) performers. In other words, competencies are any knowledge, skill, attitude, motivation, or personal characteristic that leads to successful performance.

A *competency model* is a narrative description of the requirements for success in a job, department, or organization. It is an expression of what should be. It provides a basis against which to assess individuals or groups for development, serving as a

foundation for (among other things) multi-rater, full-circle assessment; individual development planning; and career counseling. By building competencies, individuals, including WLP practitioners, can position themselves for career success (Rothwell and Lindholm, 1999).

Competencies Associated With the Role of Evaluator

Descriptions of the competencies associated with the evaluator's role can be found in Rothwell, Sanders, and Soper (1999) and are shown in table 2.1. Table 2.1 lists the competencies shared by both the analyst and evaluator roles—as well as those unique only to the evaluator. Of course, it is up to the evaluator to determine whether it may be necessary to perform some or all of the competencies shared in common.

The competencies listed in table 2.1 represent a formidable skill set. To summarize what they mean in practice, evaluators should be able to assess the value of interventions. First, evaluators should be able to look at complicated matters, breaking them down and then putting them back together in ways that can be easily understood (*analytical thinking*). Second, they should be able to make sense of evaluative data from interventions and tell what they mean, reviewing complex issues by breaking them down into meaningful components and synthesizing related items (*analyzing performance data*). Third, they should be able to compare what is happening and what should be happening so as to pinpoint additional issues for continuous improvement (*performance gap analysis*). Fourth, evaluators should be able to tell the difference between taking action and achieving desired results (*performance theory*) and clarify what results are desired (*standards identification*). Fifth, evaluators should be able to see how events are interrelated (*systems thinking*) and examine the environment surrounding the work that performers carry out to isolate issues influencing human performance (*work environment analysis*). Sixth, evaluators should be able to compare the costs of an intervention to the benefits received (*cost/benefit analysis*). Seventh, evaluators should be able to assess—and note issues for improvement—before and during interventions (*workplace performance, learning strategies, and intervention evaluation*). Eighth, evaluators should recognize trends affecting

Table 2.1: Competencies Associated with the Evaluator's Role

Competencies Unique to the Evaluator

- *Analyzing performance data:* Interpreting performance data and determining the effect of interventions on customers, suppliers, and employees
- *Cost/benefit analysis:* Accurately assessing the relative value of performance improvement interventions
- *Evaluation of results against organizational goals:* Assessing how well workplace performance, learning strategies, and results match organizational goals and strategic intent
- *Feedback:* Providing performance information to the appropriate stakeholders
- *Intervention monitoring:* Tracking and coordinating interventions to assure consistent implementation and alignment with organizational strategies
- *Knowledge capital:* Measuring knowledge capital and determining its value to the organization
- *Workplace performance, learning strategies, and intervention evaluation:* Continually evaluating and improving interventions before and during implementation

Competencies Shared By Both the Analyst and the Evaluator

- *Ability to see the "big picture":* Identifying trends and patterns that are outside the normal paradigm of the organization
- *Analytical thinking:* Breaking down complex issues into meaningful components and synthesizing related items
- *Communication:* Applying effective verbal, nonverbal, and written communication methods to achieve desired results
- *Communication networks:* Understanding the various methods through which communication is achieved
- *Interpersonal relationship building:* Interacting effectively with others in order to produce meaningful outcomes
- *Performance gap analysis:* Performing a front-end analysis by comparing actual and ideal performance levels in the workplace and identifying opportunities and strategies for performance improvement
- *Performance theory:* Recognizing the implications, outcomes, and consequences of performance interventions to distinguish between activities and results
- *Quality implications:* Identifying interrelationships and implications among quality programs and performance
- *Questioning:* Collecting data via pertinent questions in surveys, interviews, and focus groups for the purpose of performance analysis
- *Standards identification:* Determining what constitutes success for individuals, organizations, and processes
- *Systems thinking:* Recognizing interrelationships among events by determining the driving forces that connect seemingly isolated incidents within the organization; taking a holistic view of performance problems in order to find causes
- *Technological literacy:* Understanding and appropriately applying existing, new, or emerging technologies
- *Work environment analysis:* Examining the work environment for issues or characteristics that affect human performance; understanding characteristics of a high-performance workplace

Source: Rothwell, W., Sanders, E., and Soper, J. (1999). *ASTD Models for Workplace Learning and Performance: Roles, Competencies, and Outputs.* Alexandria, VA: ASTD.

performance in the organization that fall outside typical practice *(ability to see the "big picture")*, review how effectively intervention methods match up to the organization's strategic objectives *(evaluation of results against organizational goals)*, and measure and determine knowledge capital *(knowledge capital)*. Ninth, evaluators should note relationships between interventions and quality programs *(quality implications)*, use appropriate communication methods *(communication)*, understand how communication is affected by an intervention *(communication networks)*, and build good relationships that are in keeping with desired results *(interpersonal relationship building)*. Tenth and finally, evaluators must supply information about the performance of interventions to key stakeholders *(feedback)*, keep track of interventions to ensure that they are aligned with organizational strategies *(intervention monitoring)*, gather information *(questioning)*, and appropriately use emerging technology in the evaluation process *(technological literacy)*.

The Place of Evaluation in the Human Performance Improvement Process

Evaluation typically appears at the end of the HPI Process Model, the guiding model for Workplace Learning and Performance (see figure 2.1.) However, while its placement in the HPI Process Model may give the impression that it occurs last, evaluation can occur at any stage of the process. Indeed, the HPI Process Model includes formative, concurrent, and summative evaluation. *Formative evaluation* occurs before the intervention. *Concurrent evaluation* occurs during the intervention. *Summative evaluation*, perhaps the most familiar to trainers, occurs after the intervention.

Formative evaluation usually calls for small-scale pilot tests or rehearsals. These are useful to field test the effectiveness of an intervention in solving a performance problem. They also are helpful in refining the metrics for measuring results.

By definition, formative evaluation occurs before widespread implementation of an intervention. It is used to assess how well the intervention actually works in solving the performance problem. For example, evaluation at this point can be used to determine how cost-effective the intervention is and can also help identify ways to make it more cost-effective.

While formative evaluation often has been associated with training "try outs" with management or with those targeted to receive training as a way to improve instructional methods, the same logic can be applied to nonlearning interventions. For instance, if an organization's decision makers wish to solve a performance problem stemming from conflicting job responsibilities, they could choose job redesign as an intervention. However, they might wish to use a small-scale pilot test (a formative evaluation) in one part of the company rather than redesign all jobs in the organization. A small-scale pilot can help uncover the consequences of an intervention before it is implemented on a broad scale. Note that a formative evaluation of this kind focuses on examining the results of the intervention (what evaluators do) rather than focusing on solving the performance problem (what analysts do).

Concurrent evaluation requires periodic evaluations of an intervention at various milestones or checkpoints as the intervention is implemented. These periodic evaluations can help correct the course of an intervention to ensure that it reaches desired performance targets. It provides a chance to ensure continuous improvement—and to avoid the

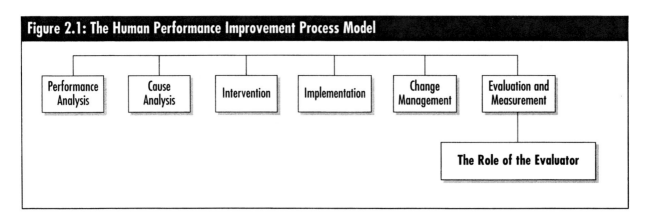

Figure 2.1: The Human Performance Improvement Process Model

Performance Analysis | Cause Analysis | Intervention | Implementation | Change Management | Evaluation and Measurement

The Role of the Evaluator

chance that an intervention can swing wildly off course.

Summative evaluation examines the results of the intervention once it is completed. Summative evaluation can loop back to analysis, leading to continuous improvement. It examines how well intervention results matched intentions, goals, or objectives and how effectively the intervention solved a performance problem revealed during the analysis process.

Outputs Associated With the Role of Evaluator

Output is the term used to refer to the results of evaluative processes. (For outputs of evaluation, see table 2.2.) However, the particular work outputs necessary in the evaluator's role depend upon the unique requirements of key stakeholders, an organization's corporate culture, and work expectations. Take a moment to consider the corporate culture and work expectations of your own organization by completing the worksheet in figure 2.2.

Table 2.2: Sample Outputs Associated with the Evaluator's Role

- ◆ Reports that show the evaluation results
- ◆ Recommendations for future WLP interventions
- ◆ Reports that determine if intervention results positively affected business objectives

Source: Rothwell, W., Sanders, E., and Soper, J. (1999). *ASTD Models for Workplace Learning and Performance: Roles, Competencies, and Outputs.* Alexandria, VA: ASTD.

Who Performs the Role of Evaluator?

The role of evaluator may be played by WLP practitioners serving as external or internal consultants, line managers, employees, or any or all of the above. Each choice of who will conduct evaluation, just like the choice of who will conduct analysis, has distinctive advantages and disadvantages.

Remember: The terms analyst and evaluator refer to roles played by people. A role is not a job title but rather a part played. Just as one person can enact several roles—such as the roles of wife, mother, daughter, niece, aunt, and worker—the roles of analyst and evaluator may be played by the same person or by different people.

External consultants often possess expertise and credibility in the subject in question, as well as experience in conducting similar evaluation studies. These are distinct advantages. Evidence of expertise such as an academic degree, a successful track record in a comparable organization, or publications authored by the external consultant on the subject may make it easier for external consultants to gain access to key stakeholders. They also may have license to ask questions or recommend approaches that otherwise might not be acceptable in the corporate culture.

External consultants may also possess disadvantages. They are not as familiar as internal consultants, line managers, or employees with an organization's corporate culture, power structure, or work processes—nor do they know the personalities or value systems of the organization's key decision makers. External consultants must find ways to familiarize themselves with such matters quickly and effectively.

Using internal consultants for evaluation studies offers certain advantages. In addition to being more familiar with the particular industry or business, the organization's corporate culture, and work processes, internal consultants can afford the time and effort to follow through on an evaluation study in a way that may not be possible for external consultants, who have other clients and other demands on their time. Clients, for example, are usually unwilling to pay for years of time for an on-site external consultant, who commands a premium rate typically much higher than internal consultants employed by the organization. Internal consultants work in the organization and thus have more staying power—and have to "live" with the results of an intervention.

Internal consultants, however, have their drawbacks as well. They may not be able to gain access to key decision makers due to a reporting structure where there may be many levels of management between internal consultants and senior decision makers. In addition, internal consultants may not be considered as credible as external consultants because they may lack the credibility gained from higher levels of education, experience, publications on relevant topics, or other features commonly considered when selecting external consultants. Further, internal consultants sometimes lack real or perceived

Figure 2.2: Worksheet to Organize Your Thinking on the Work Expectations of Your Organization for the Evaluator's Role

Directions: Use this worksheet to organize your thinking about the work expectations that your organization has for you in the role of evaluator. Remember that the role of the evaluator "assesses the impact of interventions and follows up on changes made, actions taken, and results achieved to provide participants and stakeholders with information about the effectiveness of intervention implementation" (Rothwell, Sanders, and Soper, 1999, p. xvii). However, the outputs and quality requirements of the evaluator role may vary across corporate cultures. For each competency listed under column 1 below, describe under column 2 what you believe are the expectations for results—the outputs—in your organization. (You may need to discuss this issue with the organization's key decision makers and stakeholders.) Under column 3, describe what behaviors and quality requirements would demonstrate success with that competency. What results would you have to achieve to be considered successful by your customers/stakeholders? While there are no "right" or "wrong" answers, these questions are important for building the appropriate expectations among your customers and stakeholders. Take the time to discuss these issues.

	Column 1 Competency	Column 2 What do you believe are the organization's expectations for results—the outputs —for the role of evaluator?	Column 3 What behavior and quality requirements would demonstrate success with this competency in this organization? What results would you have to achieve to be considered successful by your customers and stakeholders?
1	*Ability to see the "big picture":* Identifying trends and patterns that are outside the normal paradigm of the organization		
2	*Analyzing performance data:* Interpreting performance data and determining the effect of interventions on customers, suppliers, and employees		
3	*Analytical thinking:* Breaking down complex issues into meaningful components and synthesizing related items		
4	*Communication:* Applying effective verbal, nonverbal, and written communication methods to achieve desired results		

5	*Communication networks:* Understanding the various methods through which communication is achieved		
6	*Cost/benefit analysis:* Accurately assessing the relative value of performance improvement interventions		
7	*Evaluation of results against organizational goals:* Assessing how well work-place performance, learning strategies, and results match organizational goals and strategic intent		
8	*Feedback:* Providing performance information to the appropriate stakeholders		
9	*Interpersonal relationship building:* Interacting effectively with others in order to produce meaningful outcomes		
10	*Intervention monitoring:* Tracking and coordinating interventions to assure consistent implementation and alignment with organizational strategies		
11	*Knowledge capital:* Measuring knowledge capital and determining its value to the organization		
12	*Performance gap analysis:* Performing a front-end analysis by comparing actual and ideal performance levels in the workplace and identifying opportunities and strategies for performance improvement		

(continued on next page)

Column 1 Competency	Column 2 What do you believe are the organization's expectations for results—the outputs —for the role of evaluator?	Column 3 What behavior and quality requirements would demonstrate success with this competency in this organization? What results would you have to achieve to be considered successful by your customers and stakeholders?
13 *Performance theory:* Recognizing the implications, outcomes, and consequences of performance interventions to distinguish between activities and results		
14 *Quality implications:* Identifying interrelationships and implications among quality programs and performance		
15 *Questioning:* Collecting data via pertinent questions in surveys, interviews, and focus groups for the purpose of performance analysis		
16 *Standards identification:* Determining what constitutes success for individuals, organizations, and processes		
17 *Systems thinking:* Recognizing interrelationships among events by determining the driving forces that connect seemingly isolated incidents within the organization; taking a holistic view of performance problems in order to find causes		

Figure 2.2: Worksheet to Organize Your Thinking on the Work Expectations of Your Organization for the Evaluator's Role (continued)

18	*Technlogical literacy:* Understanding and appropriately applying existing, new, or emerging technologies		
19	*Work environment analysis:* Examining the work environment for issues or characteristics that affect human performance; understanding characteristics of a high-performance workplace		
20	*Workplace performance, learning strategies, and intervention evaluation:* Continually evaluating and improving interventions before and during implementation		

objectivity in evaluating the results of interventions, especially if they were actively involved in the implementation of the intervention. In the latter case, they may even be accused on occasion of manipulating evaluation results to make intervention results appear better than they really are.

Line managers and employees are most familiar with the results achieved by interventions—but even that familiarity has its downside. While they may know what happened as a result of an intervention, they may not possess the competencies essential to evaluate it. Of course, line managers and employees alike can be trained in the competencies of the evaluator's role, just as they can be trained in the competencies of other WLP roles.

Often the most powerful approach for evaluation is to field a team of evaluators that may include external consultants working along with internal ones, external consultants working with line managers and employees, or internal consultants working with line managers and employees.

When Do They Perform This Role?

The evaluator's role is either requested by others or initiated by evaluators themselves and is usually *situational*—in other words, it is called up in response to a particular intervention at a particular time. Too often, the evaluator's role emerges as an afterthought during a quest for after-the-fact proof to convince skeptics that an intervention was worthwhile.

It is a critically important part of the evaluator's role to convince stakeholders, before an intervention is fully under way, of the need for evaluation information. Of course, the results of a formative evaluation can be most helpful in demonstrating small-scale results. Metrics then can be refined for use when the intervention is fully implemented. But, if evaluators must scurry to develop measurement methods after the intervention is completed or is well under way, it may be difficult to secure the full buy-in of stakeholders, who already will have formed impressions about the relative value of the intervention.

When Requested by Others. WLP practitioners are familiar with occasions when they are asked to demonstrate the value of what they propose to do, are doing, or have done. Unfortunately, they often are not approached to evaluate results until after an intervention is implemented, and then it is often too late to reach agreement with key stakeholders on before-the-intervention measures of performance problem costs. Worse yet, WLP practitioners may have acted in response to an executive mandate—such as an order to deliver training—and the analysis process was reduced or ignored so that no evidence was obtained of a performance problem to be solved. As a result, it is often too late after an intervention was implemented to show that a performance problem was sufficiently addressed to warrant the intervention. In fact, there may not have been a performance problem in the first place. If a proper performance analysis was not conducted, an evaluator may be forced to repeat or doublecheck work that should have been performed earlier by an analyst.

Consider the following vignettes. Decide for yourself whether evaluation is likely to demonstrate the value of an intervention in each case.

Vignette 1: A divisional vice president orders the customer service department to extend its hours and begin offering weekend coverage. The customer service director is ordered to extend the hours without first performing a needs assessment. Months later, the director is asked to *prove* that these new hours have solved the customer satisfaction problems and should continue.

Vignette 2: "We assess our training using participant evaluations that are administered at the end of each course," explains a training director. "Unfortunately, nobody asks to see the results of these evaluations, and we don't have the time or staff to summarize the results for instructors, instructional designers, or the line managers who sent their employees to the training."

Vignette 3: "We do an annual employee attitude survey. That gives us very useful information on how well our employees believe our recruitment, selection, orientation, training, performance appraisal system, salary and incentive system, and other HR practices are working," explains the vice president of human resources. "Top managers do pay attention to employee perceptions about how well we are managing these HR matters."

As you continue reading about the evaluator's role, think about these vignettes. What questions would an evaluator ask in these situations, and how would an evaluator handle them?

When Initiated by the Evaluator. Although WLP practitioners often are prompted to enact the role of evaluator in response to requests by others, WLP practitioners also have an obligation to be proactive—that is, to evaluate the results of interventions even when they are not requested by others to do so. In these situations they are said to initiate the role of evaluator.

WLP practitioners who initiate evaluation on their own face a greater challenge than do those who simply react to the requests of others. Nobody has authorized the time, money, or staff that is necessary for the evaluation. And sometimes stakeholders view such efforts as mere grandstanding on the part of self-interested WLP practitioners who want to justify their existence.

Proactive evaluators must first find a sponsor or change champion to build awareness of the value of evaluation. And they may have to settle for after-the-fact anecdotes or success stories that provide testimonial evidence of the value of interventions (see Rothwell, 1998k).

What Is the Scope of the Projects That Evaluators Carry Out?

The term *project scope* refers to the size of the project that the evaluator carries out. Like analysis projects, evaluation projects can range in scope from the small-scale to the large-scale. In addition, projects can be carried out as either a stand-alone effort or as an effort that is integrated with other projects. The central question governing scope is this: What is the size of the group that will participate, is participating, or has participated in the intervention?

Many WLP practitioners are familiar with small-scale projects. Examples might include situations in which managers request evaluation of one training session or some other performance improvement intervention. Such projects often are carried out as one step in a process having many steps.

But the evaluator role also can be carried out as large-scale projects. Examples might include situations in which WLP practitioners are asked to evaluate a multi-year organization development intervention, the impact of a succession planning program

(Rothwell, 1994), or a career development program. In each case, evaluators may in fact be leading a long-term effort to examine the multifaceted impact of an intervention. Large-scale evaluation projects are organized around an issue to be addressed and may have a team assembled for that purpose.

One way to organize a large-scale project is to use the steps that characterize human performance analysis (see "Steps in Human Performance Analysis," 1996). When this approach is used, the evaluator

♦ **aligns** (The desired outcome is to align the client and the evaluation team on the project's focus, plan, and measures of success.)
   — Determines the business goals that the intervention was intended to achieve for the client.
   — Identifies the people who will directly affect or have affected the achievement of the goals.
   — Identifies the work-process outputs produced by the people that contribute directly to the business goals.
   — Identifies deadlines and resource constraints that affect the evaluation project.
   — Identifies data sources available to the evaluation team.
   — Establishes the project goal.
   — Selects the appropriate method of evaluation and an appropriate way to analyze the results of the evaluation study.

♦ **evaluates** (Conduct evaluation. The desired outcome is to document the factual or perceived results of the intervention as they compare to the performance problem from the analysis process that originally prompted the intervention.)
   — Verifies the process outputs produced by the target audience. Be sure to capture outputs that are out of the ordinary.
   — Collects data on the outputs, including the amount of time spent producing them, and so forth.
   — Produces a task list for each process output.
   — Collects task data, including stimuli for initiating the task, speed requirements, frequency of performance, and so forth.

♦ **reports** (The desired outcome is to create a report that will answer the questions posed by key stakeholders about the financial or nonfinancial value of the intervention.)
   — Lists in priority the targeted audience.
   — Lists in priority what information the audience wishes to receive about the intervention.
   — Selects a reporting method that will provide the information required by the stakeholders and provides what they need to make subsequent decisions.
   — Decides what additional interventions may be needed.
   — Decides how to improve the existing intervention.

A *model* helps to understand a complex object or process. An evaluation process model helps WLP practitioners and other people carry out evaluation in a systematic fashion. Each step in the model requires that action be taken. Various models for training evaluation have been proposed or described, of course (see Kirkpatrick, 1994; Minton-Eversole, 1993). So have measurement methods for other interventions (Bates, 1999). The challenge is to combine those models so that learning interventions, such as training, can be evaluated using a model that is also appropriate for nonlearning interventions, such as making improvements to employee selection, incentives and rewards, workplace design, and many others.

A Model of the Evaluation Process

Think of the evaluation process as a series of general steps as follows:

1. Determine who needs to know the evaluation results.

2. Clarify why information about the results of an evaluation is desired and what actions will be taken or what decisions will be made based on the information.

3. Ascertain how much and what kind of evidence is needed to be convincing.

4. Clarify when the evaluation of the intervention will be conducted. (This step can occur at any time before, during, and after the intervention.)

5. Verify what results are to be achieved, are being achieved, or have been achieved from the intervention.*

6. Decide how to collect and analyze information about the results of the intervention.

7. Identify present and future issues affecting the measurement of intervention results.

8. Conduct the evaluation study.

9. Report results.

10. Take actions to improve the intervention, and link the information about results back into the analysis and intervention processes.

These steps are depicted in figure 3.1, and their relationship to the evaluator's competencies is illustrated in table 3.1. This section addresses these steps and provides guidance for applying them. As you think about conducting evaluation of an intervention, use figure 4.1, "Worksheet to Guide Comprehensive Evaluation," on page 72 to help pose questions related to each step of the model.

---

*This step represents three different time frames when the evaluation should be conducted (before, during, and after the intervention). It is always recommended to do evaluation in any one, two, or all three of these time frames.

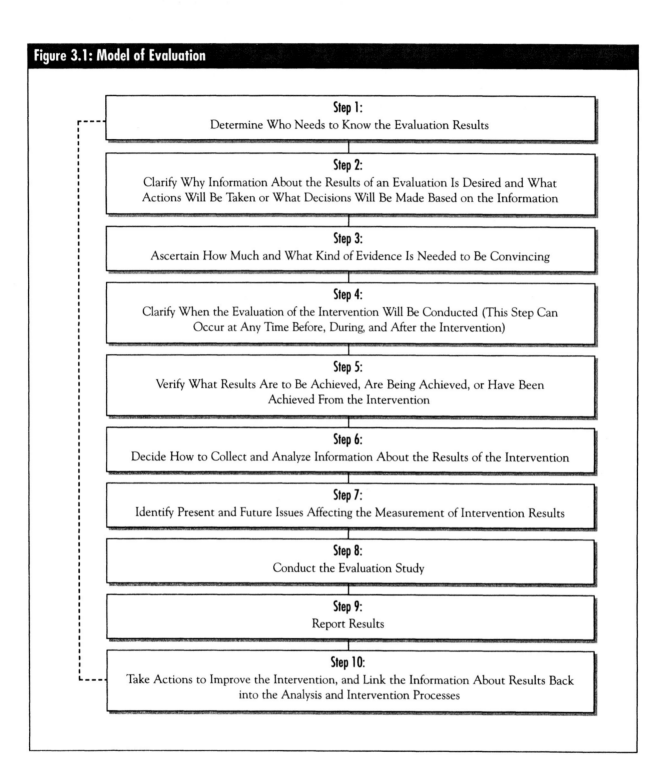

Step 1:
Determine Who Needs to Know the Evaluation Results

Step 2:
Clarify Why Information About the Results of an Evaluation Is Desired and What
Actions Will Be Taken or What Decisions Will Be Made Based on the Information

Step 3:
Ascertain How Much and What Kind of Evidence Is Needed to Be Convincing

Step 4:
Clarify When the Evaluation of the Intervention Will Be Conducted (This Step Can
Occur at Any Time Before, During, and After the Intervention)

Step 5:
Verify What Results Are to Be Achieved, Are Being Achieved, or Have Been
Achieved From the Intervention

Step 6:
Decide How to Collect and Analyze Information About the Results of the Intervention

Step 7:
Identify Present and Future Issues Affecting the Measurement of Intervention Results

Step 8:
Conduct the Evaluation Study

Step 9:
Report Results

Step 10:
Take Actions to Improve the Intervention, and Link the Information About Results Back
into the Analysis and Intervention Processes

Table 3.1: Relationship Between Evaluation and the Competencies of the Evaluator*

Model of Evaluation	Competencies of the Evaluator
Determine who needs to know the evaluation results	◆ *Analyzing performance data:* Interpreting performance data and determining the effect of interventions on customers, suppliers, and employees ◆ *Communication:* Applying effective verbal, nonverbal, and written communication methods to achieve desired results ◆ *Communication networks:* Understanding the various methods through which communication is achieved ◆ *Interpersonal relationship building:* Interacting effectively with others in order to produce meaningful outcomes ◆ *Feedback:* Providing performance information to the appropriate stakeholders
Clarify why information about the results of an evaluation is desired and what actions will be taken or what decisions will be made based on the information	◆ *Analytical thinking:* Breaking down complex issues into meaningful components and synthesizing related items ◆ *Performance gap analysis:* Performing a front-end analysis by comparing actual and ideal performance levels in the workplace and identifying opportunities and strategies for performance improvement ◆ *Performance theory:* Recognizing the implications, outcomes, and consequences of performance interventions to distinguish between activities and results ◆ *Standards identification:* Determining what constitutes success for individuals, organizations, and processes
Ascertain how much and what kind of evidence is needed to be convincing	◆ *Ability to see the "big picture":* Identifying trends and patterns that are outside the normal paradigm of the organization ◆ *Cost/benefit analysis:* Accurately assessing the relative value of performance improvement interventions ◆ *Evaluation of results against organizational goals:* Assessing how well workplace performance, learning strategies, and results match organizational goals and strategic intent ◆ *Intervention monitoring:* Tracking and coordinating interventions to assure consistent implementation and alignment with organizational strategies ◆ *Knowledge capital:* Measuring knowledge capital and determining its value to the organization ◆ *Quality implications:* Identifying interrelationships and implications among quality programs and performance ◆ *Questioning:* Collecting data via pertinent questions in surveys, interviews, and focus groups for the purpose of performance analysis ◆ *Systems thinking:* Recognizing interrelationships among events by determining the driving forces that connect seemingly isolated incidents within the organization; taking a holistic view of performance problems in order to find causes ◆ *Technological literacy:* Understanding and appropriately applying existing, new, or emerging technologies ◆ *Work environment analysis:* Examining the work environment for issues or characteristics that affect human performance; understanding characteristics of a high-performance workplace ◆ *Workplace performance, learning strategies, and intervention evaluation:* Continually evaluating and improving interventions before and during implementation

(continued on next page)

*Some competencies are used in more than one step of the model.

Table 3.1: Relationship Between Evaluation and the Competencies of the Evaluator *(continued)*

Model of Evaluation	Competencies of the Evaluator
Clarify when the evaluation of the intervention will be conducted (This step can occur before, during, and after the intervention)	◆ *Ability to see the "big picture":* Identifying trends and patterns that are outside the normal paradigm of the organization ◆ *Intervention monitoring:* Tracking and coordinating interventions to assure consistent implementation and alignment with organizational strategies ◆ *Questioning:* Collecting data via pertinent questions in surveys, interviews, and focus groups for the purpose of performance analysis ◆ *Systems thinking:* Recognizing interrelationships among events by determining the driving forces that connect seemingly isolated incidents within the organization; taking a holistic view of performance problems in order to find causes ◆ *Technological literacy:* Understanding and appropriately applying existing, new, or emerging technologies ◆ *Work environment analysis:* Examining the work environment for issues or characteristics that affect human performance; understanding characteristics of a high-performance workplace
Verify what results are to be achieved, are being achieved, or have been achieved from the intervention	◆ *Analytical thinking:* Breaking down complex issues into meaningful components and synthesizing related items ◆ *Analyzing performance data:* Interpreting performance data and determining the effect of interventions on customers, suppliers, and employees ◆ *Intervention monitoring:* Tracking and coordinating interventions to assure consistent implementation and alignment with organizational strategies ◆ *Performance gap analysis:* Performing a front-end analysis by comparing actual and ideal performance levels in the workplace and identifying opportunities and strategies for performance improvement ◆ *Performance theory:* Recognizing the implications, outcomes, and consequences of performance interventions to distinguish between activities and results ◆ *Questioning:* Collecting data via pertinent questions in surveys, interviews, and focus groups for the purpose of performance analysis ◆ *Standards identification:* Determining what constitutes success for individuals, organizations, and processes ◆ *Technological literacy:* Understanding and appropriately applying existing, new, or emerging technologies ◆ *Workplace performance, learning strategies, and intervention evaluation:* Continually evaluating and improving interventions before and during implementation

Model of Evaluation	Competencies of the Evaluator
Decide how to collect and analyze information about the results of the intervention	♦ *Analytical thinking:* Breaking down complex issues into meaningful components and synthesizing related items ♦ *Analyzing performance data:* Interpreting performance data and determining the effect of interventions on customers, suppliers, and employees ♦ *Communication:* Applying effective verbal, nonverbal, and written communication methods to achieve desired results ♦ *Communication networks:* Understanding the various methods through which communication is achieved ♦ *Cost/benefit analysis:* Accurately assessing the relative value of performance improvement interventions ♦ *Evaluation of results against organizational goals:* Assessing how well workplace performance, learning strategies, and results match organizational goals and strategic intent ♦ *Interpersonal relationship building:* Interacting effectively with others in order to produce meaningful outcomes ♦ *Intervention monitoring:* Tracking and coordinating interventions to assure consistent implementation and alignment with organizational strategies ♦ *Knowledge capital:* Measuring knowledge capital and determining its value to the organization ♦ *Performance gap analysis:* Performing a front-end analysis by comparing actual and ideal performance levels in the workplace and identifying opportunities and strategies for performance improvement ♦ *Performance theory:* Recognizing the implications, outcomes, and consequences of performance interventions to distinguish between activities and results ♦ *Quality implications:* Identifying interrelationships and implications among quality programs and performance ♦ *Questioning:* Collecting data via pertinent questions in surveys, interviews, and focus groups for the purpose of performance analysis ♦ *Standards identification:* Determining what constitutes success for individuals, organizations, and processes ♦ *Technological literacy:* Understanding and appropriately applying existing, new, or emerging technologies ♦ *Workplace performance, learning strategies, and intervention evaluation:* Continually evaluating and improving interventions before and during implementation
Identify present and future issues affecting the measurement of intervention results	♦ *Ability to see the "big picture":* Identifying trends and patterns that are outside the normal paradigm of the organization ♦ *Work environment analysis:* Examining the work environment for issues or characteristics that affect human performance; understanding characteristics of a high-performance workplace ♦ *Workplace performance, learning strategies, and intervention evaluation:* Continually evaluating and improving interventions before and during implementation

(continued on next page)

Model of Evaluation	Competencies of the Evaluator
Conduct the evaluation study	◆ *Analytical thinking:* Breaking down complex issues into meaningful components and synthesizing related items ◆ *Analyzing performance data:* Interpreting performance data and determining the effect of interventions on customers, suppliers, and employees ◆ *Cost/benefit analysis:* Accurately assessing the relative value of performance improvement interventions ◆ *Evaluation of results against organizational goals:* Assessing how well workplace performance, learning strategies, and results match organizational goals and strategic intent ◆ *Knowledge capital:* Measuring knowledge capital and determining its value to the organization ◆ *Performance gap analysis:* Performing a front-end analysis by comparing actual and ideal performance levels in the workplace and identifying opportunities and strategies for performance improvement ◆ *Performance theory:* Recognizing the implications, outcomes, and consequences of performance interventions to distinguish between activities and results ◆ *Quality implications:* Identifying interrelationships and implications among quality programs and performance ◆ *Standards identification:* Determining what constitutes success for individuals, organizations, and processes ◆ *Systems thinking:* Recognizing interrelationships among events by determining the driving forces that connect seemingly isolated incidents within the organization; taking a holistic view of performance problems in order to find causes
Report results	◆ *Communication:* Applying effective verbal, nonverbal, and written communication methods to achieve desired results ◆ *Communication networks:* Understanding the various methods through which communication is achieved ◆ *Feedback:* Providing performance information to the appropriate stakeholders ◆ *Interpersonal relationship building:* Interacting effectively with others in order to produce meaningful outcomes ◆ *Intervention monitoring:* Tracking and coordinating interventions to assure consistent implementation and alignment with organizational strategies ◆ *Questioning:* Collecting data via pertinent questions in surveys, interviews, and focus groups for the purpose of performance analysis ◆ *Technological literacy:* Understanding and appropriately applying existing, new, or emerging technologies

Model of Evaluation	Competencies of the Evaluator

Take actions to improve the intervention, and link the information about results back into the analysis and intervention processes

♦ *Cost/benefit analysis:* Accurately assessing the relative value of performance improvement interventions

♦ *Evaluation of results against organizational goals:* Assessing how well workplace performance, learning strategies, and results match organizational goals and strategic intent

♦ *Knowledge capital:* Measuring knowledge capital and determining its value to the organization

♦ *Performance gap analysis:* Performing a front-end analysis by comparing actual and ideal performance levels in the workplace and identifying opportunities and strategies for performance improvement

♦ *Performance theory:* Recognizing the implications, outcomes, and consequences of performance interventions to distinguish between activities and results

♦ *Quality implications:* Identifying interrelationships and implications among quality programs and performance

♦ *Standards identification:* Determining what constitutes success for individuals, organizations, and processes

♦ *Systems thinking:* Recognizing interrelationships among events by determining the driving forces that connect seemingly isolated incidents within the organization; taking a holistic view of performance problems in order to find causes

Step 1: Determine Who Needs to Know the Evaluation Results

Definition and Purpose of Step 1

Begin evaluation by clarifying exactly who wants the results of an evaluation study (see figure 3.2). Do not think of evaluation as an academic exercise. Realize that every evaluation study involves providing convincing evidence about the results of an intervention to one or more key stakeholder groups.

The first step in conducting evaluation is to clarify the various stakeholder groups that should want information about the intervention. It is, after all, pointless and expensive to collect information of little value to anyone. For that reason, it is essential to begin by determining who needs that information. Of course, not all stakeholders place equal value on the same information or even on the evaluation process. Some stakeholders actively and decisively seek evaluation information. Others may have to be convinced that such information is worthwhile or is worth the (possibly considerable) time, effort,

and expense necessary to collect and analyze it. Examples of possible stakeholders for evaluation include any or all of the following groups:

♦ WLP practitioners involved in analysis

♦ WLP practitioners involved in evaluation

♦ WLP practitioners enacting the role of manager

♦ Individuals or groups involved in an intervention

♦ Immediate supervisors of individuals or groups involved in an intervention

♦ Organizational policymakers and decision makers, such as top managers or stockholders

♦ The organization's customers or constituents

♦ The organization's suppliers

♦ The organization's distributors

♦ Family members of individuals participating in an intervention

♦ Government regulators, policymakers, and decision makers

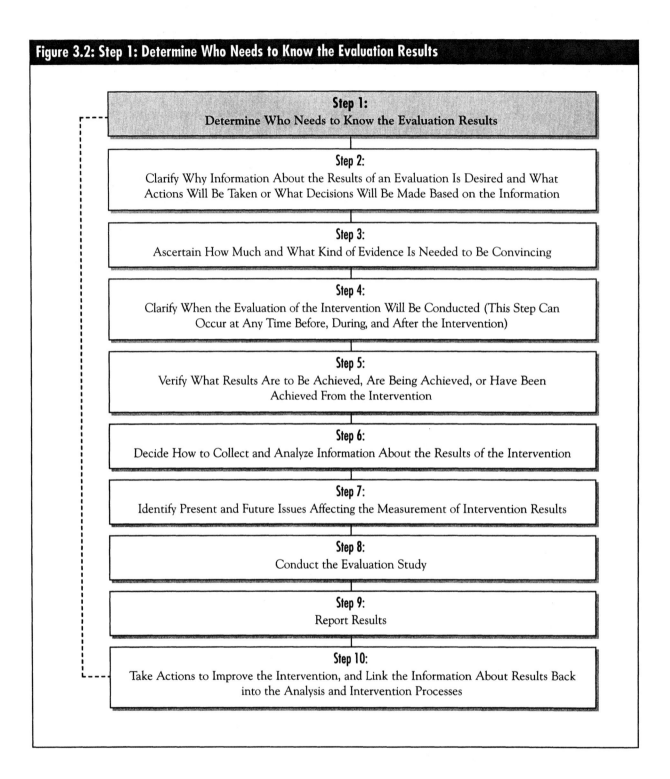

Figure 3.2: Step 1: Determine Who Needs to Know the Evaluation Results

Step 1:
Determine Who Needs to Know the Evaluation Results

Step 2:
Clarify Why Information About the Results of an Evaluation Is Desired and What Actions Will Be Taken or What Decisions Will Be Made Based on the Information

Step 3:
Ascertain How Much and What Kind of Evidence Is Needed to Be Convincing

Step 4:
Clarify When the Evaluation of the Intervention Will Be Conducted (This Step Can Occur at Any Time Before, During, and After the Intervention)

Step 5:
Verify What Results Are to Be Achieved, Are Being Achieved, or Have Been Achieved From the Intervention

Step 6:
Decide How to Collect and Analyze Information About the Results of the Intervention

Step 7:
Identify Present and Future Issues Affecting the Measurement of Intervention Results

Step 8:
Conduct the Evaluation Study

Step 9:
Report Results

Step 10:
Take Actions to Improve the Intervention, and Link the Information About Results Back into the Analysis and Intervention Processes

♦ Union officials
♦ Members of the community
♦ Other specific groups, given the nature of the intervention

Use the worksheet in figure 3.3 to identify or prioritize the relevant group(s) that may desire evaluation information and begin to organize your thinking about what information they may need.

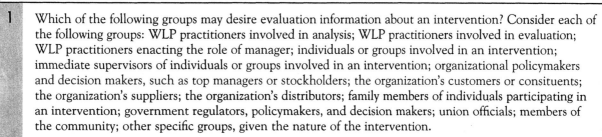

Figure 3.3: Worksheet to Identify Relevant Group(s) Desiring Evaluation Information and to Clarify What Information May Be Needed for an Intervention

Directions: Use this worksheet to help you (the evaluator) organize your thinking about what relevant groups desire evaluation information and clarify what information they may need or want.

1	Which of the following groups may desire evaluation information about an intervention? Consider each of the following groups: WLP practitioners involved in analysis; WLP practitioners involved in evaluation; WLP practitioners enacting the role of manager; individuals or groups involved in an intervention; immediate supervisors of individuals or groups involved in an intervention; organizational policymakers and decision makers, such as top managers or stockholders; the organization's customers or consituents; the organization's suppliers; the organization's distributors; family members of individuals participating in an intervention; government regulators, policymakers, and decision makers; union officials; members of the community; other specific groups, given the nature of the intervention.
2	What kind of information does each group most want to know about the results of an intervention?

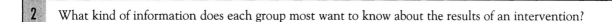

Implementing Step 1

Begin any evaluation effort by clarifying who wants to know the results of evaluation and how much interest they may have in receiving information. Consider such questions as:

♦ Who wants to know?

♦ How much do they want to know?

♦ When do they want to receive the information?

♦ In what form do they want to receive the information?

Use the Step 1 section in the worksheet in figure 4.1 to pose these and related questions about the stakeholders who want evaluation information and what kind of information they may want. If you wish, poll stakeholders on these and related issues by using the survey questionnaire appearing in figure 3.4.

Figure 3.4: Instrument for Assessing Stakeholder Opinions About the Information Desired from an Evaluation of an Intervention

Directions: This instrument is designed to gauge *your* opinions about the information you desire from an intervention evaluation. For each statement below, circle a number to the right to indicate your level of agreement. Use the following scale:

1 = Strongly Disagree
2 = Disagree
3 = Agree
4 = Strongly Agree

When you finish scoring the instrument, hand it in to the designated person and use it to clarify what information is desired from an evaluation.

		Strongly Disagree			Strongly Agree
		1	2	3	4
	The Stakeholders: Who Wants to Know?				
1	I think the people who identified the performance problem are the ones most interested in knowing what results were achieved by the intervention that was undertaken to solve the problem. *(These would be called WLP practitioners involved in analysis.)*	1	2	3	4
2	I think the people who are involved in conducting the evaluation are probably the ones most interested in knowing what results were achieved by the intervention. *(These would be called WLP practitioners involved in evaluation.)*	1	2	3	4
3	I think the manager of the training department is probably the most interested in having information abut the impact of the intervention. *(This person would be called the WLP manager.)*	1	2	3	4
4	Individuals or groups involved in an intervention are probably the ones most interested in knowing how well the intervention achieved its desired results.	1	2	3	4
5	Organizational policymakers or decision makers, such as top managers or stockholders, are probably the ones most interested in knowing how well the intervention achieved its desired results.	1	2	3	4
6	The organization's customers or constituents are probably the ones most interested in knowing how well the intervention achieved its desired results.	1	2	3	4

		Strongly Disagree			Strongly Agree
		1	2	3	4
7	The organization's suppliers are probably the ones most interested in knowing how well the intervention achieved its desired results.	1	2	3	4
8	The organization's distributors are probably the ones most interested in knowing how well the intervention achieved its desired results.	1	2	3	4
9	Family members of individuals participating in an intervention are probably the ones most interested in knowing how well the intervention achieved its desired results.	1	2	3	4
10	Government regulators, policymakers, and decision makers are probably the ones most interested in knowing how well the intervention achieved its desired results.	1	2	3	4
11	Union officials are probably the ones most interested in knowing how well the intervention achieved its desired results.	1	2	3	4
12	Members of the community are probably the ones most interested in knowing how well the intervention achieved its desired results.	1	2	3	4
13	Other groups, given the nature of the intervention, are probably the ones most interested in knowing how well the intervention achieved its desired results.	1	2	3	4
14	What groups above are the most interested in knowing the results of the intervention, and how much do they want to know? Which *single group* do you believe is most interested in receiving information about the results of the intervention, and why do you believe that one group is most interested? *(Explain.)*				
15	When do you believe the intervention stakeholders want to receive information about the results of the intervention? Do you believe they would prefer to have the most information before the intervention is implemented, during the implementation of the intervention, or after the intervention is implemented? Why?				
16	In what form do intervention stakeholders want to receive evaluation information? Would they prefer one or more oral reports, written reports, or some combination? When and how should the information be delivered?				

Vignette: A small organization, the ABC Corporation, was experiencing difficulty recruiting people for specific job categories. Chief Learning Officer Marietta Diaz was asked by company management to analyze the problem, identify its cause(s), and select and implement one or more interventions to correct the problem. Diaz determined through analysis that the company was not building sufficient awareness about the company and its possible employment opportunities among potential employees. An awareness-building campaign was therefore planned as an intervention. To build corporate visibility, company representatives would increase their visits to local schools and campuses, forge new alliances with faculty at schools from which the company had previously hired successful talent, offer salary bonuses to current workers for referrals in the targeted job categories that produced successful hires, and take other actions to improve the quantity and quality of applicant flow for the targeted job categories.

As the intervention was planned, Diaz hired consultant Martin Mulderstein to evaluate the results of the intervention. Planning for evaluation began almost at the same time that analysis was conducted. Mulderstein asked Diaz to help him identify which stakeholders were most interested in the intervention, posing the questions outlined in Step 1. By discussing the matter with key executives and other stakeholders, Mulderstein and Diaz pinpointed the people who wanted to receive information about the results of the intervention, what kind of information they wanted to receive about it, and when they wanted to know.

Step 2: Clarify Why Information About the Results of an Evaluation Is Desired and What Actions Will Be Taken or What Decisions Will Be Made Based on the Information

Definition and Purpose of Step 2

The second step in evaluation is to clarify why information about the results of an intervention is desired and what actions will be taken or what decisions will be made based on the evaluation results. (See figure 3.5.) This step may be taken whether you are trying to evaluate an intervention before, during, and after implementation.

Think of this step as intended to clarify *the desired outcomes yielded by the evaluation study.* Naturally, it is important to know what information is desired. For example, do decision makers want to know how much or how well intervention participants or other stakeholders

♦ will like, are liking, or have liked an intervention?

♦ will change, are changing, or have changed as a direct result of an intervention?

♦ will achieve, are achieving, or have achieved the desired goals or objectives for performance improvement as a direct result of an intervention?

♦ perceive that the intervention will solve, is solving, or has solved the performance problem that prompted the intervention?

♦ are likely to realize, are realizing, or have realized measurable results—both financial or nonfinancial—as a direct result of an intervention?

♦ want to know how well the intervention was planned, executed, and evaluated?

Use the questionnaire in figure 4.2 to assess participant reactions to an intervention; use the questionnaire in figure 4.3 to examine perceived changes in on-the-job behavior resulting from an intervention. Use the worksheet in figure 4.4 as one tool to examine the perceived financial results of an intervention.

Another issue to consider at this point is what decision makers plan to do or what decisions they will make based on the results of an evaluation study. Will they try to

♦ improve the intervention's management and implementation?

♦ identify new performance problems?

♦ assess how much people like the intervention?

♦ assess how much people have changed their behavior as a result of the intervention?

♦ pinpoint what factors other than the intervention that may have contributed to improvements during the intervention?

♦ quantify how much the organization gained from the intervention in improved quantity of

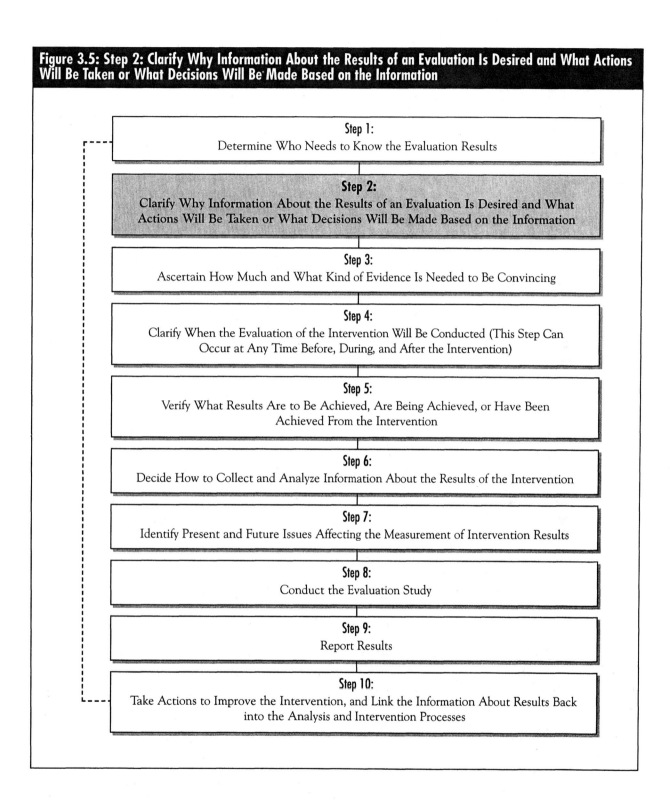

Step 1:
Determine Who Needs to Know the Evaluation Results

Step 2:
Clarify Why Information About the Results of an Evaluation Is Desired and What Actions Will Be Taken or What Decisions Will Be Made Based on the Information

Step 3:
Ascertain How Much and What Kind of Evidence Is Needed to Be Convincing

Step 4:
Clarify When the Evaluation of the Intervention Will Be Conducted (This Step Can Occur at Any Time Before, During, and After the Intervention)

Step 5:
Verify What Results Are to Be Achieved, Are Being Achieved, or Have Been Achieved From the Intervention

Step 6:
Decide How to Collect and Analyze Information About the Results of the Intervention

Step 7:
Identify Present and Future Issues Affecting the Measurement of Intervention Results

Step 8:
Conduct the Evaluation Study

Step 9:
Report Results

Step 10:
Take Actions to Improve the Intervention, and Link the Information About Results Back into the Analysis and Intervention Processes

production, reduced costs of production, improved quality of production, reduced cycle time, improved customer service, or other measures?

♦ justify the costs of the intervention based on the benefits received?

♦ determine how well an intervention has helped to close performance gaps as identified in the analysis process?

♦ identify other actions to be taken or decisions to be made based on the evaluation study results?

Implementing Step 2

To answer the question Why is information about the results of an intervention desired? begin by collecting background information about the external environment, the organization, and the intervention you are investigating. Pose such questions as these:

♦ Why do stakeholders want evaluation information, and what will they do with it once they have it?

♦ What is happening with the intervention now?

♦ Who is involved in implementing it? Who is affected by it?

♦ How has the intervention been linked to solving an important problem associated with the organization's business needs and strategic goals and objectives?

♦ How much has the performance problem been costing the organization, and how much has the intervention cost?

♦ When did the problem that the intervention was designed to correct first appear or become noticeable?

♦ Where has the problem that the intervention was designed to correct been most evident? Are there geographical differences in which the intervention is being implemented more successfully or completely in some locales than in others?

♦ What results have been obtained from the intervention?

♦ What positive and negative side effects have resulted from the intervention that were not planned but that were realized by the organization anyway?

Use the Step 2 section in the worksheet in figure 4.1 to pose these and related questions about the intervention and its impact on the problem it was designed to solve.

Vignette: ABC Corporation's Marietta Diaz began preparing for an intervention to resolve the company's recruitment problems by increasing public awareness. Before proceeding, however, consultant Martin Mulderstein and Diaz reviewed the key questions outlined in Steps 1 and 2 to identify stakeholders, assess current recruitment efforts, determine costs associated with the problem, and clarify strategic goals of the intervention among other issues.

This exercise was crucial to focusing the planning process for evaluating the results of the intervention. By posing these and similar questions, the evaluator not only clarified why stakeholders desired certain information but what actions would be taken or decisions made based on the evaluation results.

Step 3: Ascertain How Much and What Kind of Evidence Is Needed to Be Convincing

Definition and Purpose of Step 3

The next step in evaluation is to ascertain how much and what kind of evidence is needed to be convincing to the stakeholders who seek information about intervention results. (See figure 3.6.) This step, like others, is usually necessary whether you are trying to evaluate an intervention before, during, and after implementation.

Implementing Step 3

A traditional problem in evaluation has been the unfortunate tendency of some WLP practitioners to focus attention on the methods rather than the customers or stakeholders who will make decisions and take actions based on the evaluation results. Sometimes WLP practitioners become convinced that if they could only find a silver bullet for measuring results—an unassailable, methodologically rigorous approach—then they could convince critics that interventions (and particularly training interventions) have been useful.

But, in fact, there is a clear difference between *providing convincing evidence* and *proving value*

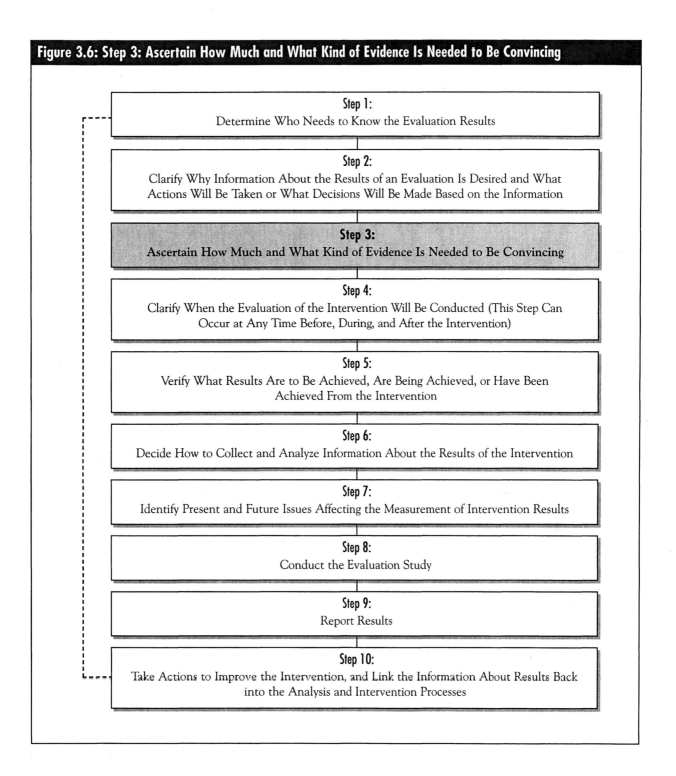

Figure 3.6: Step 3: Ascertain How Much and What Kind of Evidence Is Needed to Be Convincing

Step 1:
Determine Who Needs to Know the Evaluation Results

Step 2:
Clarify Why Information About the Results of an Evaluation Is Desired and What Actions Will Be Taken or What Decisions Will Be Made Based on the Information

Step 3:
Ascertain How Much and What Kind of Evidence Is Needed to Be Convincing

Step 4:
Clarify When the Evaluation of the Intervention Will Be Conducted (This Step Can Occur at Any Time Before, During, and After the Intervention)

Step 5:
Verify What Results Are to Be Achieved, Are Being Achieved, or Have Been Achieved From the Intervention

Step 6:
Decide How to Collect and Analyze Information About the Results of the Intervention

Step 7:
Identify Present and Future Issues Affecting the Measurement of Intervention Results

Step 8:
Conduct the Evaluation Study

Step 9:
Report Results

Step 10:
Take Actions to Improve the Intervention, and Link the Information About Results Back into the Analysis and Intervention Processes

(Rothwell, Hohne, and King, 2000). As any good lawyer knows, for instance, a jury can be supplied with convincing evidence. But a legal case is not *proved* until the jury *believes* that evidence. The same principle holds true in evaluating interventions. If stakeholders do not believe the evidence with which they are presented, then the value of intervention results is not demonstrated—even when methods are precise, measurement methods are valid and reliable, and the evaluation design matches first-rate research methods. In other words, using elegant statistical tests or having a methodologically sound research design for an evaluation study may satisfy purists and academic researchers, but they are not adequate—and often are not even appropriate—to convince managers or other stakeholder groups.

This step in evaluation, then, requires WLP practitioners or others who perform evaluation to determine precisely *what evidence* and *how much evidence* will be necessary to convince the jury of stakeholders that an intervention yielded useful results. The level of evidence required may range from highly valid, reliable, and methodologically sound research methods (see figure 3.7) to less valid, reliable, and methodologically sound research methods. In short, the level of evidence required to be convincing varies by the stakeholders who need to be convinced and the credibility of those conducting the evaluation study.

To address this issue, consider such questions as these:

♦ What kind of evidence will be necessary to convince each stakeholder group? How much rigor and precision is needed, and how will that be judged?

♦ How much should the stakeholders be actively involved in the design, data collection, and analysis of evaluation results to find the study's results persuasive?

♦ How much evidence will be necessary to be convincing and credible to each stakeholder group?

♦ In what form should the evidence be presented to be most useful to each stakeholder group?

Figure 3.7: Primer on Research Methods

While much has been written about research, the essence of research is clarifying what you want to find out before you do so. While research has a bad name in some business circles because it is sometimes associated with answering useless questions, the fact is that nothing is more practical than good research. It helps to uncover new opportunities, underscore areas for improvement, and uncover past successes (as well as past failures). Conducting evaluation is much like conducting research, though the primary difference is that evaluation is usually associated with examining the results of efforts while research can be undertaken merely to satisfy idle curiosity.

Key steps in conducting any research study include:

1. Clarifying the background of the problem or issue being investigated. (What led up to the study?)

2. Stating clearly and specifically the problem or issue to be investigated.

3. Stating
   A. hypotheses to be tested
   B. research questions to be answered
   C. research objectives to be achieved
   D. dependent and independent variables to be assessed in the study
   E. how special terms are to be operationally defined
   F. what assumptions were made by researchers when conducting the study
   G. what limitations may have existed in conducting the study.

4. Providing information about background research literature relevant to the problem, hypotheses, research questions, and research objectives.

5. Describing the methods to be carried out during the study, including
   A. how and why the data collection method was chosen
   B. how various authorities, who have written about the research methods to be used, have recommended that the method should be used (for instance, how surveys should be conducted, how focus groups should be conducted, how interview studies should be conducted)

C. how the study will be conducted step-by-step

D. how samples will be selected and why it is appropriate to select them

E. how results will be analyzed and why those analytical methods are appropriate.

6. Providing the results of the study so as to

    A. provide the results of the data collected

    B. answer research questions

    C. meet research objectives

    D. provide the results of hypotheses that were tested.

7. Providing

    A. a summary of the study

    B. conclusions based on the results

    C. recommendations for follow-up studies to examine issues raised by the research study.

Use the Step 3 section in the worksheet in figure 4.1 to pose these and related questions about the amount and kind of evaluation evidence that will prove most useful and convincing to key stakeholders.

Vignette: In planning the evaluation study of the intervention to improve recruitment methods at ABC Corporation, Martin Mulderstein met individually with key stakeholders who stood to gain from the intervention, as well as with people who would participate. In a focus group he posed the questions to them provided in this section. From the results of the focus group, he learned that stakeholders—primarily middle managers—simply wanted to know whether the intervention had improved the number of qualified applicants for the targeted job categories at ABC Corporation. They requested to see monthly statistics of how many applicants were being attracted to ABC Corporation from each group included in the intervention and from other sources (such as responses to newspaper and Web-based advertising), and they wanted to see how those statistics compared to other organizations in the area, as well as ABC Corporation statistics at the same time the previous year. They believed that the evidence would be most convincing if a third-party consultant like Mulderstein collected the data. They also asked to see summaries of how many applicants were actually hired from those who applied and the chief reasons why applicants were not selected once they did apply.

Step 4: Clarify When the Evaluation of the Intervention Will Be Conducted (This Step Can Occur Before, During, And After the Intervention)

Definition and Purpose of Step 4

The fourth step in evaluation is to clarify at what stage(s) of the intervention the evaluation is to be conducted. (See figure 3.8.) Should it be done before the intervention, during the intervention, after the intervention, or at all of the stages? This is an important question because its answer can influence the resources committed to evaluation and therefore the costs of doing evaluation work.

Implementing Step 4

Recall that evaluation can be performed before, during, and after interventions. It is important to clarify early on when the evaluation should be conducted, since each type of evaluation is usually intended to serve a different purpose.

Typically, formative evaluation is intended to refine or improve an intervention before widespread implementation. While formative evaluations of training programs are perhaps best-known, they also may be conducted for other kinds of interventions. Such evaluations go by many names—including alpha tests, beta tests, pretests, pilot tests, rehearsals, or even rapid prototyping projects.

Formative evaluations of training programs usually begin with individual testing (Rothwell and Kazanas, 1998). Individuals from the group targeted

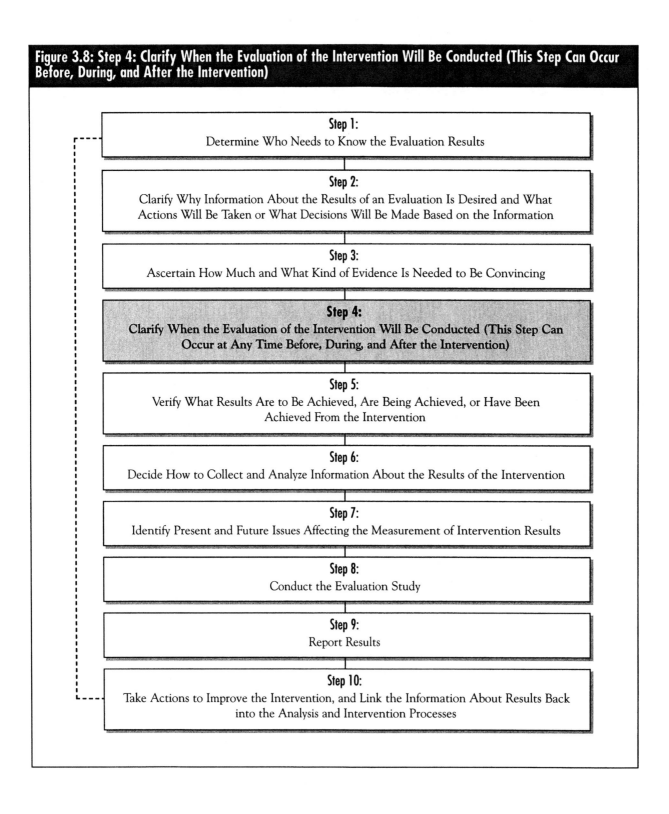

Figure 3.8: Step 4: Clarify When the Evaluation of the Intervention Will Be Conducted (This Step Can Occur Before, During, and After the Intervention)

Step 1:
Determine Who Needs to Know the Evaluation Results

Step 2:
Clarify Why Information About the Results of an Evaluation Is Desired and What Actions Will Be Taken or What Decisions Will Be Made Based on the Information

Step 3:
Ascertain How Much and What Kind of Evidence Is Needed to Be Convincing

Step 4:
Clarify When the Evaluation of the Intervention Will Be Conducted (This Step Can Occur at Any Time Before, During, and After the Intervention)

Step 5:
Verify What Results Are to Be Achieved, Are Being Achieved, or Have Been Achieved From the Intervention

Step 6:
Decide How to Collect and Analyze Information About the Results of the Intervention

Step 7:
Identify Present and Future Issues Affecting the Measurement of Intervention Results

Step 8:
Conduct the Evaluation Study

Step 9:
Report Results

Step 10:
Take Actions to Improve the Intervention, and Link the Information About Results Back into the Analysis and Intervention Processes

to receive training sit down with trainers and review training materials to ensure that they are clear. These individuals are asked for their opinions about which instructional materials should be improved and how they can be improved. Attitude surveys also may be administered to assess how much participants liked the training materials and methods, and tests on the material also may be given to determine how much the participants learned from it.

Formative evaluations of training programs may then be extended to include small-group testing with other trainers, immediate supervisors of the targeted participants, or members of the group targeted for training. Of course, each stakeholder group can offer different advice for improving instruction. For instance, trainers can provide advice about what training methods to use; immediate supervisors can provide advice about the subject matter, its applicability to the organization, and ways to reinforce training before and after people participate in it; and members of the group targeted for training can provide suggestions for ways to improve the clarity of materials. Subsequent formative evaluations of training also may be conducted in the field—that is, close by the work settings of targeted participants—to improve the chance for successful transfer of learning (Rothwell and Kazanas, 1998). Figure 3.9 provides systematic guidance for conducting a formative evaluation of training.

Formative evaluation also may be conducted with nonlearning interventions. Such interventions may include making improvements to recruitment, selection, incentives and rewards, tools and equipment, workspace design, job or organizational design, or other factors falling under management control. Formative evaluations of this kind typically are called pilot tests and may involve small groups of people. Such people may be hand-picked to find those who are most likely to succeed or who possess favorable attitudes toward the intervention. (This technique is called *cherry picking,* and its goal is usually to improve the chance that the intervention will score a quick, early success.) These hand-picked people can help to improve and refine the intervention before it is unveiled in large systems where results may be less predictable, less controllable, and slower than in small-scale pilot tests. Figure 3.10 provides

detailed guidelines for conducting a formative evaluation of nonlearning interventions.

It should be noted, however, that the trend in business has been to reduce or entirely eliminate the use of formative evaluation in the traditional sense. One reason is that it delays the implementation of the intervention on a broad scale. More common now is the use of *rapid prototyping* in which training or a nonlearning intervention is designed, delivered, and then (in real time) improved based on initial experiences. Rapid prototyping tends to slash development time, though it can also have a downside when imperfect (half-baked) interventions lead to loss of credibility for WLP practitioners.

Concurrent evaluation occurs during the intervention. The methods for conducting concurrent evaluation of training programs may include quizzes, experiential small-group activities such as case studies or role plays that require participants to demonstrate that they know how to apply what they have learned, and periodic "process checks" in which trainers ask participants directly and explicitly how well they feel the training is meeting their needs. Figure 3.11 provides suggestions for carrying out concurrent evaluations of training.

The methods for conducting concurrent evaluation of nonlearning interventions follow the same basic principles used with training. Concurrent evaluation is therefore carried out as interventions are implemented. Examples of data-gathering methods that might be used for concurrent evaluation of this kind can include focus group meetings, off-site retreats to focus attention on the direction of the intervention, or attitude-survey questionnaires distributed to participants or other stakeholders involved in the intervention. The goal of such evaluations is usually to track the progress of an intervention to ensure it stays on target. Figure 3.12 provides suggestions for carrying out concurrent evaluations of nonlearning interventions.

Summative evaluation occurs after the intervention. The methods for conducting summative evaluation of training interventions include participant questionnaires to assess how much participants liked the training; tests of knowledge, skills, or performance carried out at the end of training; on-the-job follow-up studies with participants or their supervisors

Figure 3.9: Systematic Guidance for Conducting a Formative Evaluation of Training

Step	What to Do
1.	Finalize the training material so that it is as close as possible to the form in which it should be presented to the targeted audience.
2.	Select specific individuals to participate in the formative evaluation. Be clear who should attend, such as A. experienced workers B. exemplary performers C. immediate supervisors of the targeted participants D. supervisors of immediate supervisors (middle or top managers, for example) E. other groups (customers, suppliers, distributors, or other stakeholders, for example).

3.	Decide
	
	A. The exact purpose of the formative evaluation, including the relative priorities of
	    ♦ testing the clarity of the materials
	    ♦ testing the clarity of the methods
	    ♦ examining how much participants
	        — like the training
	        — learn from the training
	        — are likely to transfer changed behavior back to their jobs
	        — feel the training will lead to improved (and measurable) productivity, profitability, reduced costs, improved service, improved customer service, or other desirable goals
	    ♦ examining the likely impact of the training on
	        — targeted participants as *individuals*
	        — *groups* of targeted participants
	        — individuals in off-the-job settings
	        — individuals in on-the-job settings
	        — immediate supervisors of targeted participants
	        — other relevant stakeholder groups
	B. how data will be collected and analyzed to improve the training materials and methods
	C. when and where the formative evaluation study will be conducted
	D. how revisions will be made to the materials based on participant input.

4.	Carry out the evaluation by A. opening the formative evaluation by explaining its purpose, goals, and objectives B. explaining why the participants were chosen and what they might gain from their participation C. reviewing the training materials and methods D. collecting participants' insights and opinions E. writing down and organizing participants' insights and opinions.
5.	Follow up on the evaluation by improving training materials and methods to be consistent with the purpose and goals of the formative evaluation study.

Figure 3.10: Systematic Guidance for Conducting a Formative Evaluation of Nonlearning Interventions

Step	What to Do
1.	Finalize the plan for the nonlearning intervention and prepare a step-by-step description of what it is and why it will be conducted (that is, what performance problem it was intended to solve and the cost or other impacts of that problem).
2.	Select specific individuals to participate in the formative evaluation. Be clear who should attend, including A. experienced workers B. exemplary performers C. immediate supervisors of the targeted participants in the intervention D. supervisors of immediate supervisors (such as middle or top managers)? E. other groups (such as customers, suppliers, distributors, or other stakeholders).
3.	Decide A. The exact purpose of the formative evaluation, including the relative priorities of ◆ testing the clarity of the materials to be used in the nonlearning intervention ◆ testing the clarity of the methods to be used in the nonlearning ntervention ◆ examining how much participants — like the intervention — believe they will change from the intervention — perceive the intervention will solve the problem that prompted it — feel the intervention will lead to measurable improvements in productivity, profitability, operating costs, product or service quality, improved customer service, or other desirable goals ◆ examining the impact of the proposed nonlearning intervention on — targeted participants as *individuals* — *groups* of targeted participants — individuals in off-the-job settings — individuals in on-the-job settings — immediate supervisors of targeted participants — other relevant stakeholder groups B. how data will be collected and analyze to improve the nonlearning intervention materials and methods C. when and where the formative evaluation will be conducted D. how revisions will be made to the materials based on participant input.
4.	Carry out the evaluation by A. opening the formative evaluation by explaining its purpose, goals, and objectives B. explaining why the participants were chosen and what they might gain from their participation C. reviewing the nonlearning intervention plan, materials, and methods D. collecting participants' insights and opinions about the intervention plan, materials, and methods E. writing down and organizing the participants' insights and opinions.
5.	Follow up on the evaluation by improving the plan, materials, and methods associated with the nonlearning intervention to make them consistent with the purpose and goals of the formative evaluation study.

Figure 3.11: Suggestions for Carrying Out Concurrent Evaluations of Training

Step	What to Do
1.	Finalize the plan, materials, and methods for the training and prepare a step-by-step description of why the concurrent evaluation will be conducted
2.	Select who will participate in the concurrent evaluation from among the following groups, including A. experienced workers B. exemplary performers C. immediate supervisors of the participants in the intervention D. supervisors of immediate supervisors (such as middle or top managers) E. other groups (such as customers, suppliers, distributors, or other stakeholders).
3.	Decide A. the exact purpose of the concurrent evaluation, including the relative priorities of ♦ testing how much participants — like the training as it is delivered — are learning during the training — are being prepared for on-the-job behavior change as a result of the training — are being positioned to help the organization achieve results from the training—including measurable improvements in productivity, profitability, operating costs, improved product or service quality, or other desirable goals ♦ examining the impact of the training as it is being delivered and as it is appropriate on — targeted participants as *individuals* — *groups* of targeted participants — individuals in off-the-job settings — individuals in on-the-job settings — immediate supervisors of targeted participants — other relevant stakeholder groups B. how data will be collected and analyzed to evaluate training as it is being delivered C. when the concurrent evaluation will be conducted D. how the results of the concurrent evaluation will be used.
4.	Carry out the concurrent evaluation by A. explaining the purpose, goals, and objectives of any and all methods chosen for concurrent evaluation and inform participants and other relevant stakeholders of them B. implementing the evaluation C. providing feedback to participants and other stakeholders about the results of concurrent evaluation.
5.	Follow up on the concurrent evaluation by improving the training materials and methods.
6.	Provide recommendations to relevant stakeholders about the results of concurrent training evaluation and anything they can do to improve the impact of training results while the training is being delivered.

Figure 3.12: Suggestions for Carrying Out Concurrent Evaluations of Nonlearning Interventions

Step	What to Do
1.	Finalize the plan for the concurrent evaluation and prepare a step-by-step description of how it will be conducted.
2.	Select who will participate in the concurrent evaluation, including A. experienced workers B. exemplary performers C. immediate supervisors of the participants in the intervention D. supervisors of immediate supervisors (such as middle or top managers) E. other groups (such as customers, suppliers, distributors, or other stakeholders).
3.	Decide A. the exact purpose of the concurrent evaluation, including the relative priorities of ◆ assessing how much participants and other relevant stakeholders — like the nonlearning intervention as it is implemented — are changing on-the-job behavior as it is implemented — are being positioned to help the organization achieve results from the nonlearning intervention—including measurable improvements in productivity, profitability, operating costs, product or service quality, or other desirable goals ◆ examining the impact of the nonlearning intervention as it is being implemented and as it is appropriate on — targeted participants as *individuals* — *groups* of targeted participants — individuals in off-the-job settings — individuals in on-the-job settings — immediate supervisors of targeted participants — other relevant stakeholder groups B. how data will be collected and analyzed to evaluate the nonlearning intervention as it is being implemented C. when the concurrent evaluation will be conducted D. how the results of the concurrent evaluation will be used.
4.	Carry out the concurrent evaluation by A. explaining the purpose, goals, and objectives of any and all methods chosen for concurrent evaluation and inform participants and other relevant stakeholders about them B. implementing the evaluation C. providing feedback to participants and other stakeholders about the results of concurrent evaluation.
5.	Follow up on the concurrent evaluation by improving the materials and methods of the nonlearning intervention.
6.	Provide feedback to all other relevant stakeholders about the results of concurrent nonlearning intervention evaluation and anything they can do to improve the nonlearning intervention as it is being implemented.

to assess behavioral change occurring on the job; and return-on-investment studies intended to determine how much an intervention yielded in financial benefits minus intervention costs. Summative evaluation has been the focus of considerable attention in recent years as trainers work to demonstrate that their efforts have added value and have successfully closed gaps in deficiencies of knowledge, skill, or attitude influencing individual performance. Figure 3.13 provides suggestions for carrying out summative evaluations of training interventions.

Of course, summative evaluation can also be focused on nonlearning interventions. To do that most effectively, WLP practitioners or others should carefully establish measurable performance objectives before the intervention is implemented. Results can then be tracked against pre-established, measurable performance objectives that describe what problem is to be solved by the intervention and how success in solving that problem will be measured. Elaborate evaluation designs may be created or else less rigorous methods may be used. (See figure 3.14 for a description of a way to carry out a summative evaluation of a nonlearning intervention.)

To successfully carry out this step, WLP practitioners or others responsible for evaluation should address such questions as these:

♦ When should the evaluation be conducted?

♦ Why should the evaluation be carried out at the time selected?

♦ How should the evaluation study be carried out?

♦ How much time, staff, money, and other resources are decision makers willing to provide to conduct the evaluation study at the times desired?

Use the Step 4 section in the worksheet in figure 4.1 to pose these and related questions about how to clarify the time when the intervention will be conducted.

Vignette: Martin Mulderstein, as part of his consulting for ABC Corporation, asked key stakeholders when they would like to have the evaluation study conducted. Should it be done before the intervention, during the intervention, or after the intervention? As part of that effort, Mulderstein also asked key stakeholders to review possible project plans for each type of evaluation study, as well as the time, money, staff, and other

requirements necessary to conduct each type of evaluation study. Although the stakeholders initially requested evaluation information at all stages, they finally decided to request concurrent evaluations on a monthly basis and a final summary report upon the anniversary of the intervention's launch. Their decision was based on the information supplied by Mulderstein about the resources required to evaluate the intervention before, during, and after implementation.

Step 5: Verify What Results Are to Be Achieved, Are Being Achieved, or Have Been Achieved From the Intervention

Definition and Purpose of Step 5

The fifth step in evaluation is to determine what results were to be achieved from the intervention. (See figure 3.15.) What measurable outcomes were desired from it? This step answers that question. It is a very important background question, and it is in answering this question that evaluators approach many issues that were also examined by analysts in an earlier stage of the HPI process model.

Implementing Step 5

Begin by verifying what results are to be achieved from the intervention by clarifying the desired results that were identified during the analysis process. Review the work previously performed by analysts to clarify who is involved in performance, what they do, how they do it, when they do it, and what others say about the results achieved. If this work wasn't already accomplished during the analysis process, conduct this work now. As in analysis, this step begins by clarifying the environment in which performance is achieved. Recall that examples of issues associated with the performance environment include:

♦ The status of the economy and of global competition

♦ The organization's strategic goals and objectives

♦ Top managers' ability to exert leadership and guide the organization

♦ The organization's command structure and organizational scheme

♦ The department's goals and objectives

Figure 3.13: Suggestions for Carrying Out Summative Evaluations of Training Interventions

Step	What to Do
1.	Finalize a plan to evaluate training after it has been delivered.
2.	Select who will participate in the summative evaluation, including A. participants in the training B. immediate supervisors of the participants C. supervisors of immediate supervisors (such as middle or top managers) E. other groups (such as customers, suppliers, distributors, or other stakeholders).
3	Decide A. the exact purpose of the evaluation, including the relative priorities of finding out how much the training ♦ solved the performance problem(s) leading up to it ♦ met the expectations of key stakeholders ♦ was liked by participants ♦ prompted learning for participants ♦ led to on-the-job behavior change for participants ♦ led to measurable improvements in organizational productivity, profitability, operating costs, product or service quality, customer satisfaction, or other desirable goals B. how data will be collected and analyzed to evaluate training results C. when and where the summative evaluation will be conducted D. how improvements will be made to the training E. how measurable results will be effectively communicated to the participants and stakeholders of the training intervention.
4.	Carry out the evaluation by A. explaining the purpose, goals, and objectives of the summative evaluation B. explaining why the participants in the summative evaluation were chosen and what they might gain from their participation C. collecting and analyzing the evaluation information D. organizing the evaluation information.
5.	Follow up on the evaluation by improving the plan, materials, and methods associated with the training in line with the results of the intervention.
6.	Report the results of the summative evaluation to the stakeholders who want to receive the information and in a form they prefer.

♦ The department managers' ability to exert leadership

♦ The department's command structure and organizational scheme

♦ The work group's or team's goals and objectives

♦ The supervisor's ability to exert leadership

♦ The work group's or team's command structure and organizational scheme

♦ The individual's job duties and expectations

In each case, these issues focus around the environment in which people perform. They also influence the success of an intervention.

Figure 3.14: Ways to Carry Out Summative Evaluations of Nonlearning Interventions

Step	What to Do
1.	Finalize a plan to evaluate a nonlearning intervention once it has been implemented.

2. Select who will participate in the summative evaluation, including

    A. participants in the interventions

    B. immediate supervisors of the participants in the intervention

    C. supervisors of immediate supervisors (such as middle or top managers)

    E. other groups (such as customers, suppliers, distributors, or other stakeholders).

3. Decide

    A. the exact purpose of the evaluation, including the relative priorities of finding out how much the intervention

       ◆ solved the performance problem(s) leading up to it

       ◆ met the expectations of key stakeholders

       ◆ was liked by participants

       ◆ led to on-the-job behavior change for participants

       ◆ led to measurable improvements in organizational productivity, profitability, operating costs, product or service quality, customer satisfaction, or other desirable goals

    B. how data will be collected and analyzed to evaluate the results of the nonlearning intervention

    C. when and where the summative evaluation will be conducted

    D. how improvements will be made to the nonlearning intervention based on the evaluation results

    E. how measurable results will be effectively communicated to the participants and other stakeholders involved with or affected by the nonlearning intervention.

4. Carry out the evaluation by

    A. explaining the purpose, goals, and objectives of the summative evaluation

    B. explaining why the participants in the summative evaluation were chosen and what they might gain from their participation

    C. collecting the evaluation information about the nonlearning intervention

    D. organizing the evaluation information.

5. Follow up on the evaluation by improving the plan, materials, and methods associated with the nonlearning intervention to be consistent with the purpose and goals of the intervention.

6. Report the results of the summative evaluation to the stakeholders who want to receive the information and in a form they prefer.

Figure 3.15: Step 5: Verify What Results Are to Be Achieved, Are Being Achieved, or Have Been Achieved from the Intervention

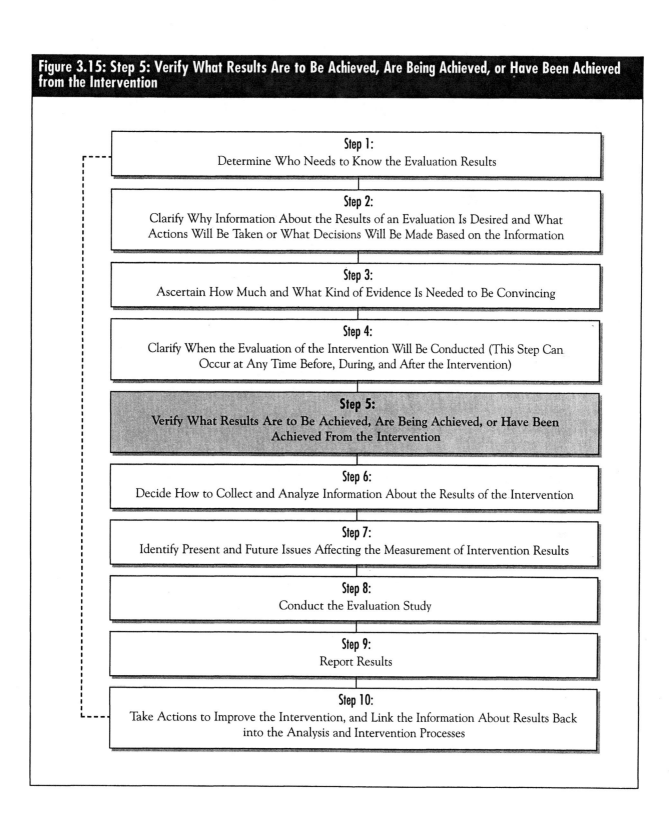

Step 1:
Determine Who Needs to Know the Evaluation Results

Step 2:
Clarify Why Information About the Results of an Evaluation Is Desired and What Actions Will Be Taken or What Decisions Will Be Made Based on the Information

Step 3:
Ascertain How Much and What Kind of Evidence Is Needed to Be Convincing

Step 4:
Clarify When the Evaluation of the Intervention Will Be Conducted (This Step Can Occur at Any Time Before, During, and After the Intervention)

Step 5:
Verify What Results Are to Be Achieved, Are Being Achieved, or Have Been Achieved From the Intervention

Step 6:
Decide How to Collect and Analyze Information About the Results of the Intervention

Step 7:
Identify Present and Future Issues Affecting the Measurement of Intervention Results

Step 8:
Conduct the Evaluation Study

Step 9:
Report Results

Step 10:
Take Actions to Improve the Intervention, and Link the Information About Results Back into the Analysis and Intervention Processes

Next, answer the question What is the performance environment in which the intervention was or is being carried out? Conduct an organizational analysis or diagnosis to help you answer this question. Use such questions as these to guide the organizational analysis or diagnosis of the intervention:

♦ How clearly do people understand the performance expected of them in the intervention, and how much agreement exists among people that such performance is desirable?

♦ How well can experienced performers recognize the situations in which they are expected to perform during the intervention (that is, *identify performance cues*)?

♦ How often do people receive feedback on their performance during the intervention, how clear is the feedback they receive, and in what forms do they receive feedback?

♦ What tools, equipment, and other resources are absolutely essential to performance during the intervention, and how many people have those available when they are needed?

♦ How often do people confront decisions or situations for which they believe higher authority is needed for a decision during an intervention, and how often is that access really necessary and available when needed?

♦ How organized are the work processes of the intervention?

♦ In what ways are people provided with incentives for performing during the intervention and rewarded for performing after the intervention? Do they see what is in it for them?

♦ How much do people value the rewards they receive and believe that the performance required to achieve those rewards during the intervention is fair, capable of achievement, and will result in the promised rewards?

♦ How willing are people to make bold (even risky) decisions to satisfy customers and achieve results through new, possibly untried methods during the intervention?

If you wish, poll employees on these and related issues by using the survey questionnaire appearing in figure 3.16.

Next, evaluators should clarify exactly what results were desired or were optimal from the intervention. This stage has to do with clarifying *criteria* for the intervention, defined as the optimal or most desirable state (Rothwell, 1998b). Examples of criteria include:

♦ Organizational policy

♦ Organizational procedures

♦ Customer expectations, either explicitly stated or implicitly derived from practice

♦ Industry practice

♦ Best practice

♦ Laws, regulations, or ordinances

♦ Management values or expectations

♦ A vision statement

♦ Job descriptions

♦ Collective bargaining agreements

♦ Work standards or expectations

♦ Productivity levels of the best performers (*exemplars*)

In each case, these issues focus on desirable or optimal results from the intervention. They represent ideals to be achieved.

In many cases, clarifying criteria for an intervention can be helpful in its own right and can serve as a human performance improvement intervention. The reason: Evaluators sometimes discover that stakeholders, decision makers, or other interested parties do not share a common understanding—or are not necessarily in agreement—about the desirable results of an intervention. That can happen on occasion due to *goal displacement* in which an intervention was undertaken to solve one problem but ends up as a catchall to solve other problems that it was never originally intended to solve.

Assessing Desired Results

To answer the question What results are desired from an intervention as identified by the analysis? pose such questions as these:

♦ What issues or trends in the work environment call for new action? In short, where are competitive conditions headed and why?

Figure 3.16: Instrument for Measuring the Performance Environment in Which the Intervention Was Carried Out

Directions: Use this instrument to measure perceptions about the performance environment in which the intervention was carried out. For each item in the left column, circle a number in the right column to measure what you perceive about the performance environment. Use the following scale:

1 = Strongly Disagree
2 = Disagree
3 = Agree
4 = Strongly Agree

When you finish scoring the instrument, refer to the Scoring section at the end of the instrument.

	Perceptions of the Performance Environment in Which the Intervention Was Carried Out	Strongly Disagree 1	2	3	Strongly Agree 4
1	People clearly understand the performance expected of them in the intervention.	1	2	3	4
2	There is broad agreement among people involved in the intervention that the performance expected of them is desirable.	1	2	3	4
3	Experienced performers recognize the situations in which they are expected to perform during the intervention.	1	2	3	4
4	People receive frequent feedback on their performance during the intervention.	1	2	3	4
5	People receive clear feedback on their performance during the intervention.	1	2	3	4
6	People receive feedback on their performance during the intervention in forms appropriate to achieving improved results.	1	2	3	4
7	People possess the tools, equipment, and other resources that are absolutely essential to successful performance during the intervention.	1	2	3	4
8	People have timely access to the tools, equipment, and other resources that are absolutely essential to successful performance during the intervention.	1	2	3	4
9	During an intervention people do not frequently confront decisions or situations for which they believe higher authority is needed for a decision.	1	2	3	4
10	People have access to higher authority during an intervention when it is really needed.	1	2	3	4
11	The work processes of the intervention are organized well.	1	2	3	4
12	People are provided with appropriate incentives for performing in ways consistent with the intervention during the intervention.	1	2	3	4

(continued on next page)

Figure 3.16: Instrument for Measuring the Performance Environment in Which the Intervention Was Carried Out *(continued)*

	Perceptions of the Performance Environment in Which the Intervention Was Carried Out	Strongly Disagree 1	2	3	Strongly Agree 4
13	People are provided with appropriate rewards for performing in line with the objectives of the intervention.	1	2	3	4
14	People recognize the benefits of performing in ways prescribed by the intervention's objectives.	1	2	3	4
15	People value the rewards they receive to achieve results in line with interventions.	1	2	3	4
16	People believe that the performance required to receive rewards during an intervention is fair, capable of achievement, and will result in the promised rewards.	1	2	3	4
17	People are likely to make bold (even risky) decisions to satisfy customers and achieve results through new, possibly untried methods during the intervention.	1	2	3	4

Add up the scores from columns 1-17 and insert the sum in the box at right:

Scoring

If your score on this instrument was between 17 and 34, then:	The performance environment has not supported the intervention. It is doubtful that decision makers were genuinely committed to it.
If your score on this instrument was between 35 and 68, then:	The performance environment was only somewhat supportive of the intervention. Specific action should have been taken by key decision makers and stakeholders to create an environment that supported the intervention.
If your score was 69 or greater, then:	The performance environment has been very supportive of the intervention. Decision makers have demonstrated a genuine commitment to success and have been willing to assemble the resources to make the intervention work.

◆ What are the performance differences between the best-performing organizations in the industry, and how does their performance (as measured by return on equity or numerous other measures) compare to that of the organization in which the analysis is conducted?

◆ What is the difference between the highest-performing and the lowest-performing work units and individuals? What accounts for those differences?

◆ How should the organization provide guidance to performers about what is expected of them, and how should disagreements be resolved?

◆ What key business issues are affecting this organization? Which ones are most important, and why are they most important?

◆ How profitable is the organization now? How profitable should it be in the future? What are the goals for profitability?

- What return on investment (ROI) and return on equity (ROE) is the organization realizing now? What are its goals in those areas? (If it is a large organization, what parts of the business are realizing the greatest ROI and ROE, and why exactly are those parts more successful than others?)

- What is the organization's targeted market share? How was that target established, and how realistic is it?

- What are the targets for quality? What error rates have been targeted? How realistic are those targets, and have they ever been achieved?

- What are the targets for customer satisfaction? How have those been identified, measured, and tracked? What feedback is given about customer satisfaction to performers, and how much should they be receiving?

About an Intervention

- What should be happening, and what results or outcomes are desired?

- Who should be involved to make that happen?

- How will the realization of the intervention's goal help meet the organization's business needs and achieve strategic goals and objectives?

- When are these desired results to be achieved? Over what time span?

- What interim goals or milestones could be achieved over time toward realizing the ultimate goal?

- What does the "optimal state" look like? What will be happening when it is achieved? What results will be obtained?

- What steps have already been taken to create a vision or spell out the desirable results to be achieved, and what level of agreement among decision makers has been reached on those?

Vignette: As a next step in the evaluation project for ABC Corporation, Martin Mulderstein asked key stakeholders what results were to be achieved from the intervention. He reviewed the analysis performed by ABC Corporation Chief Learning Officer Marietta Diaz. However, he wanted to assess—independent of her findings during the analysis process—what results decision makers sought from the intervention.

With Diaz's help, he formed a steering committee comprising people from a broad cross section of the organization. In the first meeting of that committee, he asked members the key questions outlined in Step 5 to assess desired results and to determine intervention parameters.

Mulderstein's goal in asking these questions was to check for the clarity of the goals of the intervention and the level of agreement that various stakeholder groups had with achieving these goals. As Mulderstein explained to Diaz, "I realize that you already have conducted analysis, determined the cause of the problem, and selected an intervention that you believed would solve the problem. But, I simply need to check whether the intervention goals are clear, since it is difficult to achieve desired results—or evaluate them—when people do not know for sure what they want or do not agree with those goals."

Mulderstein's questions revealed that the committee agreed with the choice of the intervention and were clear what results should be obtained from it.

Step 6: Decide How to Collect and Analyze Information About the Results of the Intervention

Definition and Purpose of Step 6

The sixth step in evaluation is to decide how to collect information about the results of the intervention and over what time frame to measure factual or perceived outcomes. (See figure 3.17.) This step involves choosing a data collection approach and appropriate analytical methods.

Implementing Step 6

Begin this step by considering different approaches to collecting information. (See figure 3.18 for an overview of data collection approaches.) While the aim in this module is not to teach the intricacies of survey research design, interviewing methods, or other approaches, evaluators will need to select a method for collecting data that will yield information of value to stakeholders. The question is What data collection method is most likely to do that?

Of course, the choice of a data collection method is closely related to the choice of analytical methods. Would stakeholders prefer that the results be presented in numbers (quantitative results?), in words (qualitative results?), or in some combination of

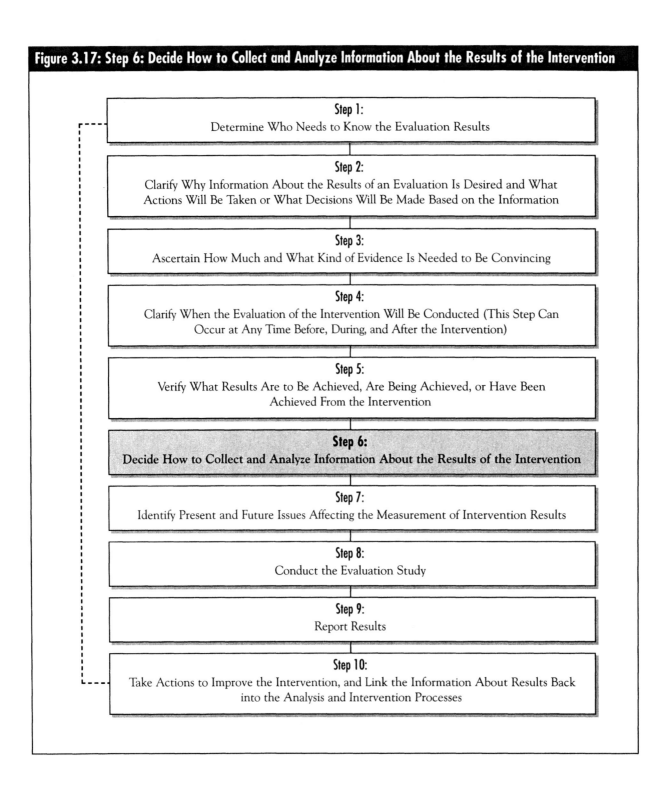

Figure 3.17: Step 6: Decide How to Collect and Analyze Information About the Results of the Intervention

Step 1:
Determine Who Needs to Know the Evaluation Results

Step 2:
Clarify Why Information About the Results of an Evaluation Is Desired and What Actions Will Be Taken or What Decisions Will Be Made Based on the Information

Step 3:
Ascertain How Much and What Kind of Evidence Is Needed to Be Convincing

Step 4:
Clarify When the Evaluation of the Intervention Will Be Conducted (This Step Can Occur at Any Time Before, During, and After the Intervention)

Step 5:
Verify What Results Are to Be Achieved, Are Being Achieved, or Have Been Achieved From the Intervention

Step 6:
Decide How to Collect and Analyze Information About the Results of the Intervention

Step 7:
Identify Present and Future Issues Affecting the Measurement of Intervention Results

Step 8:
Conduct the Evaluation Study

Step 9:
Report Results

Step 10:
Take Actions to Improve the Intervention, and Link the Information About Results Back into the Analysis and Intervention Processes

Figure 3.18: Data Collection Methods to Use in Evaluating Interventions

Directions: Read down the column to the left. For each topic you find there, read under the title for each row opposite the topic for additional information.

Method	What It Is	How To Use It	Advantages	Disadvantages
Written Questionnaires	Administer a written attitude survey to participants immediately following an intervention	Clarify what participant reactions are important before preparing an instrument	Fast to administer	Written questionnaires are mistakenly used as a sole tool for measuring reactions
	Administer a written attitude survey to participants and their immediate supervisors or peers some time after an intervention to assess on-the-job behavior change resulting from the intervention	Prepare a written draft	Easy to administer	Low response rates
		Ask others to review it	If anonymous, individuals feel free to express their true feelings without undue group experience	
		Administer a written attitude survey to participants immediately following an intervention		
Interviews	Talk to participants individually immediately after the intervention	Prepare a list of questions to be asked of all respondents in advance	Permits individualized give-and-take that written surveys do not	May be expensive if participants in an intervention are geographically separated
	Talk to participants individually and their immediate supervisors or peers some time after the intervention	Prepare an outline to guide the interview	Interviewers can follow up with questions and probe for information	Can be time-consuming and expensive to plan and carry out
		Decide whether questions will be scaled or open-ended		

(continued next page)

Figure 3.18: Data Collection Methods to Use in Evaluating Interventions *(continued)*				
Method	**What It Is**	**How To Use It**	**Advantages**	**Disadvantages**
Phone Surveys	Administer an attitude survey to participants over the phone	Same as written questionnaires	Saves the travel expense associated with interviews	Individuals are difficult to reach by phone
	Administer an attitude survey to participants and their immediate supervisors or peers over the phone some time after the intervention		Permits the give-and-take of an interview	It may be difficult to reach all or most of the participants in an intervention
			Permits personal contact	The interviewer does not see body language
			Allows for probing and follow-up questions in a way that written questionnaires do not	Respondents become impatient with lengthy discussions
Focus Groups	Ask the participants in an intervention and their direct supervisors for their reactions immediately after intervention	Limit the questions to 2-3 in 30-minute time frame	Allows face-to-face discussion and interaction of all participants	Face-to-face discussions can lead some individuals to dominate the discussion, creating false conclusions that are not representative of a group
	Call together the participant group for a debrief on the intervention during implementation and some time after the intervention was conducted	Use follow-up questions with participants in the focus group	Fast	Limited in the quantity of information that can be obtained
		Choose whether to conduct immediately after the intervention or some time afterward	Permits group members to glean ideas from each other	
		Decide whether to include peers and supervisors as well as participants in the intervention		

numbers and words? Why do they want the results presented in the form that they do? Surveys, interviews, focus groups, and other data collection methods can be scaled to yield quantitative results (such as means, medians, modes, standard deviations, and even lend themselves to other statistical tests), can be prepared to prompt narrative responses that will yield qualitative results (which can be analyzed through content analysis), or a combination of both.

In carrying out this step, evaluators should pose such questions as these:

♦ When should information be collected about the results of the intervention?

♦ How should that information be collected? What methods or data collection approaches should be used, and what systematic approach can help to guide the data collection process?

♦ How should the data be analyzed, and why are those analytical methods most appropriate for the stakeholders targeted to receive those data?

Use the Step 6 section in the worksheet in figure 4.1 to pose these and related questions about issues affecting how to conduct the evaluation study.

Vignette: As part of his preparation for evaluating the results of the nonlearning intervention to be carried out by ABC Corporation, Mulderstein continued his work with the steering committee. He asked the members of the committee to answer the questions outlined in Step 6.

While Mulderstein did receive some varying opinions from members of the committee in response to these questions, committee members agreed that the data should be collected quantitatively. They wanted to see simple numerical summaries of how many people applied for the targeted positions, when they applied, and how the applicant flow varied over time.

Step 7: Identify Present and Future Issues Affecting the Measurement of Intervention Results

Definition and Purpose of Step 7

The seventh step in evaluation is to identify present and future issues affecting the measurement of intervention results. (See figure 3.19.) How will conditions outside the organization, inside the organization, and with the intervention change over time and thereby affect the measurement process? That is the key issue to be examined in this step.

Implementing Step 7

Neither performance problems nor intervention results remain static. Like everything else, change is the only constant. Measuring intervention results, like analyzing performance problems, is akin to "shooting at a moving target" (Rothwell and Kazanas, 1993). For that reason, an important question for evaluators to consider is How will the measurable impact of the intervention change over time?

To carry out Step 7, an evaluator considers factors that will change the measurable impact of the intervention—much like analysts use environmental scanning to consider factors that will change the measurable impact of a problem. Recall that *environmental scanning* is the process of examining an organization's external environment and identifying trends that may influence the performance of the organization, work group, or individual in the future. When applied to evaluation, environmental scanning is uniquely targeted to detect changes in the future impact of the intervention. It is important for evaluation because environmental scanning permits evaluators to examine possible changes in the impact of interventions.

Environmental scanning for evaluation requires WLP practitioners or others to (a) classify the external environment into sectors; (b) decide on a time horizon appropriate for measurement; (c) examine external environmental sectors for expected changes over the time horizon that has been chosen; and (d) infer the likely measurable effects of environmental changes on the intervention.

First, classify the external environment into sectors. There are many ways to identify and classify sectors in the external environment that may influence the intervention. Examples of such sectors might include:

♦ *Economic conditions*—that is, conditions having to do with the business cycle and the relative climate for the organization in a nation, region, or globally, including preferences of both individual and institutional consumers

♦ *Political conditions*—that is, having to do with the relative climate that politics creates for the organization in a nation, region, or globally

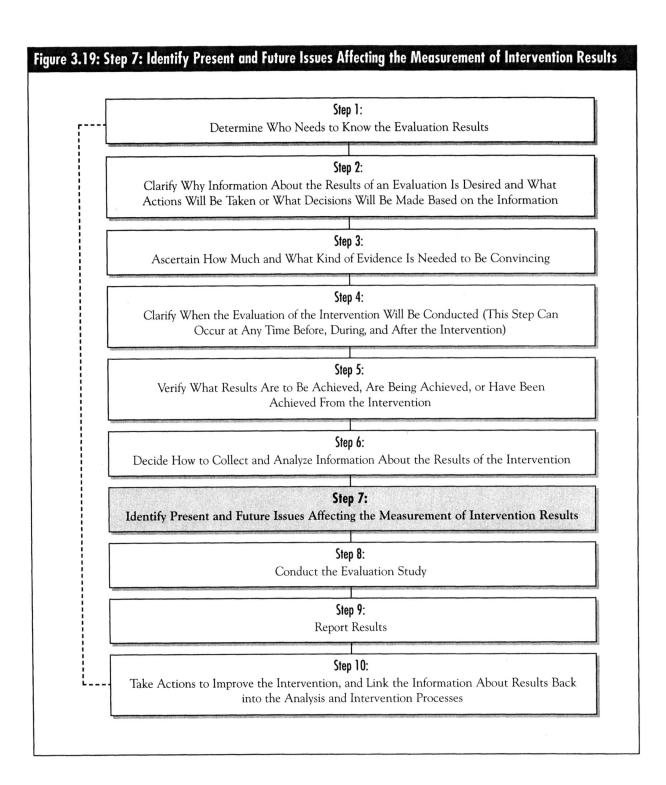

Figure 3.19: Step 7: Identify Present and Future Issues Affecting the Measurement of Intervention Results

Step 1:
Determine Who Needs to Know the Evaluation Results

Step 2:
Clarify Why Information About the Results of an Evaluation Is Desired and What Actions Will Be Taken or What Decisions Will Be Made Based on the Information

Step 3:
Ascertain How Much and What Kind of Evidence Is Needed to Be Convincing

Step 4:
Clarify When the Evaluation of the Intervention Will Be Conducted (This Step Can Occur at Any Time Before, During, and After the Intervention)

Step 5:
Verify What Results Are to Be Achieved, Are Being Achieved, or Have Been Achieved From the Intervention

Step 6:
Decide How to Collect and Analyze Information About the Results of the Intervention

Step 7:
Identify Present and Future Issues Affecting the Measurement of Intervention Results

Step 8:
Conduct the Evaluation Study

Step 9:
Report Results

Step 10:
Take Actions to Improve the Intervention, and Link the Information About Results Back into the Analysis and Intervention Processes

- *Legal/regulatory conditions*—that is, having to do with laws, regulations, and rules affecting the organization in a nation, region, or globally

- *Social conditions*—that is, having to do with social mores and opinions and the relative climate they create for the organization in a nation, region, or globally

- *Market conditions*—that is, having to do with the business market and the relative climate it creates for the organization in a nation, region, or globally

- *Competitors inside the industry*—that is, those already doing business in the industry

- *Competitors outside the industry*—that is, those that are not yet doing business in the industry but are capable of either entering the industry or developing replacement technologies

- *Suppliers*—that is, individuals or other entities that supply the organization with its raw materials and necessary provisions

- *Distributors*—that is, individuals or organizations that distribute or transport the organization's product or otherwise help the organization reach its targeted customers

- *Geographic conditions*—that is, having to do with the location of key materials, suppliers, distributors, or customers

- *Technological conditions*—that is, having to do with tools, equipment, and work processes

Another way to classify the environment to examine the likely changes that will affect an intervention is to focus special attention on key trends that are most likely to exert influence over the workforce and workplace of the future (Rothwell, Prescott and Taylor, 1998). For a given intervention the evaluator may pose the following questions:

- What trends outside the organization have affected the intervention most as it was implemented?

- What trends outside the organization are likely to affect the intervention in the future?

- How have factual or perceived results of the intervention changed over time, and how might those results change in the future?

- How might these changes in conditions outside the intervention affect the results of the intervention as measured by how much stakeholders like it, have seen change resulting from it, or realized measurable gains from it?

Second, decide on a time horizon. In other words, how far into the future will the scanning encompass? How far into the future do stakeholders wish to assess the value of an intervention? In answering these questions, evaluators should remember that the longer the time span for the scanning effort, the less likely it is to be accurate.

Third, examine external environmental sectors for expected changes over the time horizon that has been chosen. What changes have occurred outside the organization as the intervention was implemented, and what changes are expected to occur in the future that may influence the results obtained from the intervention? In short, what is the best guess about the impact of an intervention over the time horizon that has been chosen? To answer this last question, evaluators may want to discuss these issues with stakeholders of the intervention and consult external consultants familiar with the industry.

Fourth and finally, infer the likely measurable effects of environmental changes on the intervention. Draw conclusions about the likely impact of external factors on the intervention as it was implemented. If necessary, collect information from stakeholders about how much influence they perceived to have been exerted on the intervention by factors outside the organization and about how much influence they expect those factors outside the organization to exert on the intervention in the future.

Use the Step 7 section in the worksheet in figure 4.1 to consider present and future issues affecting the measurement of intervention results.

Vignette: Consultant Martin Mulderstein talked to committee members representing a broad cross section of the organization, along with ABC's Marietta Diaz, about issues that might change the impact of the intervention as it was being implemented. Of particular interest was the question, How will the measurable impact of the intervention change over time?

Committee members were asked to scan the environment for future changes that might influence the intervention's results. Mulderstein asked them to consider questions regarding economic, political, legal/regulatory, social, and market conditions, as well as competitors, suppliers, distributors, and technological trends affecting their industry.

Mulderstein also asked committee members to decide on a time horizon for the evaluation, examine external environmental sectors for expected changes over the time horizon that has been chosen, and infer the likely measurable effects of environmental changes on the intervention. Based on the results of this step, committee members agreed that they believed that few conditions would influence the intervention in the short term (about one year). However, they encouraged Mulderstein to monitor any major unexpected changes and report them to the committee.

Step 8: Conduct the Evaluation Study

Definition and Purpose of Step 8

The eighth step in evaluation is to conduct the evaluation study. (See figure 3.20.) It involves implementing the intervention evaluation project plan and collecting information about the impact of the intervention.

Implementing Step 8

While conducting an evaluation study of an intervention may appear to be a straightforward process, it rarely turns out to be as easy as it seems. Many problems will occur during the implementation of the project plan that will affect results. It is worth considering these problems. Among the most common and the most difficult to manage are:

- Insufficient resources applied to the evaluation study
- Key stakeholders changing during the evaluation study
- New issues involving the intervention discovered during the evaluation that were unknown at the time the evaluation study was planned
- Difficulty collecting desired information

Insufficient resources applied to the evaluation study means that during project planning evaluators underestimated the time, money, people, or other resources needed to carry out the study. To solve that problem, improve estimation methods during project planning. It may be necessary, however, to request additional resources from decision makers to finish the study.

Changes in key stakeholders during the evaluation study means that the people who want the evaluation results—that is, the client or stakeholders—change as the evaluation study is conducted. For instance, the company may experience a change in chief executive officer, chief learning officer, or line managers. Such changes will usually require evaluators to discuss with the new stakeholders what information they require from the evaluation study. It may also necessitate making midcourse corrections to the project plan guiding the evaluation to capture the information desired by new clients or stakeholders.

Evaluators may find problems or issues that they did not expect when they planned the study. For example, suppose the organization is implementing a new pay plan and that intervention is intended to solve problems with recruitment and retention. Suppose that the organization also introduced radical modifications to employee benefits that affect employees' real or perceived total compensation. The change to the benefit plan would introduce a whole new series of issues that would have to be considered during the evaluation of the pay plan intervention. To deal with this issue, evaluators may need to modify their evaluation project plan to include new areas for examination. As an alternative, and with the permission of key stakeholders, they could choose not to examine the impact of the change in the benefit plan. (That is called a *limitation* of the evaluation study.)

Difficulty collecting desired information is perhaps the most common barrier encountered during the information-gathering stage. If evaluators conduct a survey, for instance, the response rate may be disappointingly low. If they conduct a focus group, they may find that fewer participants than they expected show up—or else the wrong people show up. While some of these problems may seem unusual, they share a common theme of difficulty in collecting the desired information. One way to avoid such problems is to anticipate them during project planning and attempt to use proven methods to increase response rate or ensure participation.

Figure 3.20: Step 8: Conduct the Evaluation Study

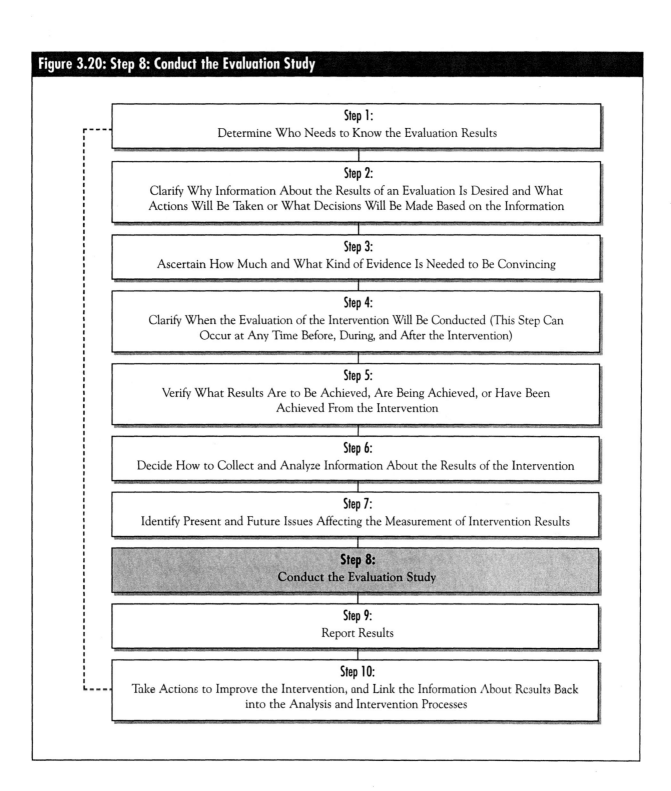

Step 1:
Determine Who Needs to Know the Evaluation Results

Step 2:
Clarify Why Information About the Results of an Evaluation Is Desired and What Actions Will Be Taken or What Decisions Will Be Made Based on the Information

Step 3:
Ascertain How Much and What Kind of Evidence Is Needed to Be Convincing

Step 4:
Clarify When the Evaluation of the Intervention Will Be Conducted (This Step Can Occur at Any Time Before, During, and After the Intervention)

Step 5:
Verify What Results Are to Be Achieved, Are Being Achieved, or Have Been Achieved From the Intervention

Step 6:
Decide How to Collect and Analyze Information About the Results of the Intervention

Step 7:
Identify Present and Future Issues Affecting the Measurement of Intervention Results

Step 8:
Conduct the Evaluation Study

Step 9:
Report Results

Step 10:
Take Actions to Improve the Intervention, and Link the Information About Results Back into the Analysis and Intervention Processes

A few questions to ask during this step include:

♦ How well does the project plan work in practice as it is implemented?

♦ During the evaluation study, is it apparent that insufficient resources were applied to doing the study?

♦ During the evaluation study, did key stakeholders change? Was the evaluation study design reconsidered in light of the possible new information needs of new stakeholders?

♦ During the evaluation study, were issues discovered that involved the intervention that were unknown at the time the evaluation study was planned? How were those issues handled?

♦ Was there difficulty collecting the desired information as the evaluation study was conducted? If so, how was that issue addressed?

Use the Step 8 section in the worksheet in figure 4.1 to pose these and related questions about issues affecting how to conduct the evaluation study.

Vignette: Once Martin Mulderstein had reached agreement with the steering committee at ABC Corporation about all preceding steps, he was ready to conduct the evaluation study. Marietta Diaz implemented the intervention, and Mulderstein began tracking it immediately. He assembled the information requested by the stakeholders and provided periodic reports independent of Diaz. (Diaz also received a copy.)

Several practical problems surfaced during the evaluation study of the intervention. First, several members of the steering committee resigned or were reassigned to new duties during the one year period in which the evaluation study was conducted. New issues surfaced. Questions were raised about the company's exit interview methods, which could have been a useful source of information about the reasons why members of the group targeted for the intervention resigned. Mulderstein also encountered difficulty verifying the information he received from company representatives as they visited campuses and took other steps to improve recruitment methods because they resisted additional paperwork. This information was reported to committee members

and provided the basis for corrective action even as the intervention was implemented and as the evaluation study was conducted.

Step 9: Report Results

Definition and Purpose of Step 9

A critical step in evaluation process is to report the results of the evaluation study. (See figure 3.21.) While the reporting approach should have been planned in an earlier step, it is at this time that evaluators prepare a written or oral report for key stakeholders to provide them with the intervention results.

Implementing Step 9

Evaluators should be able to take action on this step easily if they have clarified (as they should have done at an earlier stage) who will want the results of the evaluation study and what kind of information they will require.

The results of an evaluation study may, of course, be presented through an oral presentation, through a formal or informal written report, or through a combination of these methods. Such a report should at least be clearly prepared, minimize the time requirements of the listener or reader, and provide the information required by key stakeholders. It may also answer any of the following questions:

♦ What was the intervention, and what performance problem was it intended to solve as identified from the analysis process? (This information may be obtained from the analyst's notes if a proper analysis was conducted.)

♦ What was happening before the intervention was implemented, and what evidence existed to indicate the nature, cost, and scope of the performance problem? (Likewise, this information should be available from the analyst's notes.)

♦ How was the intervention carried out, by whom, at what locations, using what methods, and over what time?

♦ What stakeholders wanted to receive information about the results of the intervention, what kind of information did they want to receive, and how were they polled for their preferences?

Figure 3.21: Step 9: Report Results

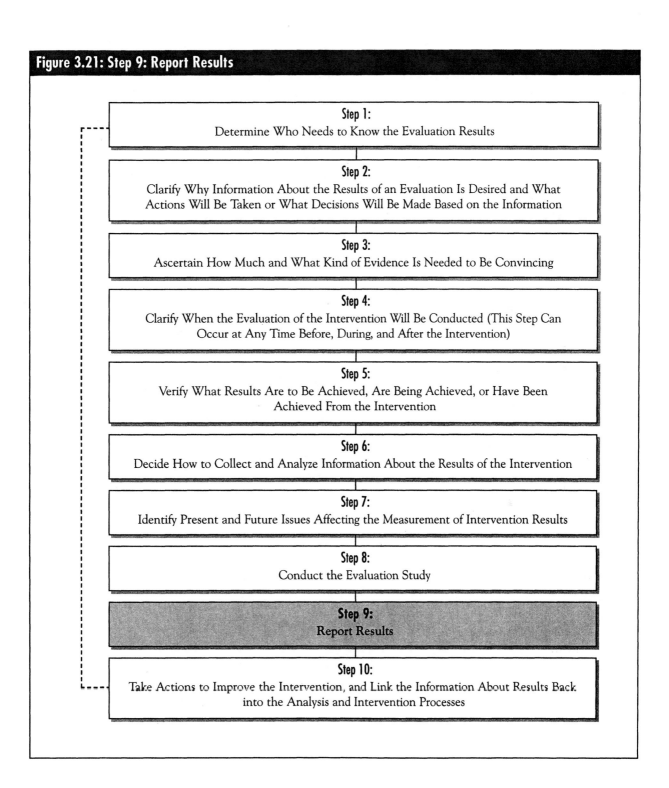

Step 1:
Determine Who Needs to Know the Evaluation Results

Step 2:
Clarify Why Information About the Results of an Evaluation Is Desired and What Actions Will Be Taken or What Decisions Will Be Made Based on the Information

Step 3:
Ascertain How Much and What Kind of Evidence Is Needed to Be Convincing

Step 4:
Clarify When the Evaluation of the Intervention Will Be Conducted (This Step Can Occur at Any Time Before, During, and After the Intervention)

Step 5:
Verify What Results Are to Be Achieved, Are Being Achieved, or Have Been Achieved From the Intervention

Step 6:
Decide How to Collect and Analyze Information About the Results of the Intervention

Step 7:
Identify Present and Future Issues Affecting the Measurement of Intervention Results

Step 8:
Conduct the Evaluation Study

Step 9:
Report Results

Step 10:
Take Actions to Improve the Intervention, and Link the Information About Results Back into the Analysis and Intervention Processes

- How was the evaluation study carried out, by whom, at what locations, using what methods, and over what time?

- What was happening after the intervention was implemented, and what evidence existed to indicate the nature, benefits, and scope of the intervention?

- What problems arose during the evaluation study, and how were they addressed?

- What was the measurable difference between the performance problem as it existed before the intervention and its current status after the intervention? (This information may be gleaned from the analyst's notes if a proper analysis was conducted.)

- What factors outside the control of evaluators may have influenced the outcomes of the evaluation study, and how much influence did they have on the results?

- What future factors might affect future benefits received from the intervention?

- What recommendations could be made for improving the intervention in the future?

Figure 3.22 depicts a checklist of issues that should be addressed in an evaluation report. That checklist also can be useful in structuring an evaluation report to the stakeholders.

Use the Step 9 section in the worksheet in figure 4.1 to consider issues that may involve the reporting of results of the evaluation study.

Vignette: Consultant Martin Mulderstein met periodically with committee members during the intervention to review outcomes and to help Marietta Diaz monitor results against the performance problem that the recruitment intervention was intended to solve. The company's efforts seemed to pay off: applicant flow increased, resignations among workers in the targeted job categories decreased, and selection ratios also increased. Data collected from other organizations indicated that ABC Corporation was more effectively attracting applicants than other organizations in the local area.

Mulderstein provided monthly reports as stakeholders requested. He limited the report to one page to minimize the time requirements demanded of the readers, and the committee members provided favorable feedback about the form in which the information was presented.

Figure 3.22: Checklist of Issues That Should Be Addressed in an Evaluation Report

Directions: Use this checklist to help you structure your thinking about issues that should be included in an evaluation report. For each question posed in the left column below, provide an answer in the right column.

Question *Does the report contain*	Answer			
	Yes	**No**	**Not Applicable**	**Comments**
1 A digest or summary? If so, does this explain	( )	( )	( )	
A why the report was requested?	( )	( )	( )	
B what intervention was evaluated?	( )	( )	( )	
C what results the intervention sought to achieve?	( )	( )	( )	
D how the intervention was implemented?	( )	( )	( )	
E who requested the evaluation?	( )	( )	( )	
F when the evaluation was conducted?	( )	( )	( )	
G how the evaluation was conducted?	( )	( )	( )	
H who conducted the evaluation?	( )	( )	( )	
I what the major results or findings of the evaluation were?	( )	( )	( )	
J what should be done as a result of the evaluation to improve the intervention?	( )	( )	( )	
2 A background section? If so, does this explain briefly	( )	( )	( )	
A why the intervention was implemented?	( )	( )	( )	

(continued next page)

Question		Answer			
Does the report contain		**Yes**	**No**	**Not Applicable**	**Comments**
B	what performance problems the intervention was intended to solve?	( )	( )	( )	
C	how the intervention was implemented?	( )	( )	( )	
D	where the intervention was implemented?	( )	( )	( )	
E	special problems confronting the intervention?	( )	( )	( )	
F	who is responsible for the intervention?	( )	( )	( )	
3	an evaluation section? If so, does this explain briefly	( )	( )	( )	
A	what, specifically, was to be evaluated?	( )	( )	( )	
B	how the matter for evaluation was identified?	( )	( )	( )	
C	relevant criteria, if appropriate?	( )	( )	( )	
D	the research or evaluation design used, if appropriate?	( )	( )	( )	
E	any limitations on the results as a consequence of the design?	( )	( )	( )	
F	major assumptions made in the evaluation?	( )	( )	( )	
G	what data collection method was selected?	( )	( )	( )	
H	why the data collection method was selected?	( )	( )	( )	
I	how data were collected?	( )	( )	( )	
J	how data were organized?	( )	( )	( )	

Question	Answer			
Does the report contain	Yes	No	Not Applicable	Comments
K how data were analyzed?	( )	( )	( )	
L why data were analyzed as they were?	( )	( )	( )	
4 a findings section? If so, does this explain:	( )	( )	( )	
A intervention results?	( )	( )	( )	
1 in terms of participant reactions?	( )	( )	( )	
2 in learning, if appropriate?	( )	( )	( )	
3 in terms of behavioral change?	( )	( )	( )	
4 in terms of productivity increases?	( )	( )	( )	
5 in terms of other outcomes as appropriate?	( )	( )	( )	
B differences between results and criteria?	( )	( )	( )	
C differences between results and the objectives governing the intervention?	( )	( )	( )	
D economic value of intervention impact less intervention cost and methods of computation shown?	( )	( )	( )	
E projected future savings or reduced costs resulting from the intervention?	( )	( )	( )	
F side effects of the intervention (planned or unplanned), how determined, and how assessed?	( )	( )	( )	

(continued next page)

Figure 3.22: Checklist of Issues That Should Be Addressed in an Evaluation Report *(continued)*					
Question		**Answer**			
Does the report contain		Yes	No	Not Applicable	Comments
5	a recommendations section? If so, does this explain	( )	( )	( )	
A	how the findings should be used to improve the intervention in the future?	( )	( )	( )	
B	how the findings should be used to improve other interventions in the future?	( )	( )	( )	
C	how the findings should be communicated and to whom?	( )	( )	( )	
D	how the findings may impact on other interventions?	( )	( )	( )	
E	other (*Specify:*)				

Source: Rothwell and Sredl. (1992). *The ASTD Reference Guide to Professional Human Resource Development Roles and Competencies, Vol. II.* Amherst, MA: Human Resource Development Press.

Step 10: Take Actions to Improve the Intervention, and Link the Information About Results Back into the Analysis and Intervention Processes

Definition and Purpose of Step 10

The final step in the evaluation process is to take action to improve the intervention and bring the process full circle. (See figure 3.23.) This step ensures continuous improvement of interventions, underscoring areas for possible improvement in it or other interventions. This step typically is taken after stakeholders have received the report containing the results of the evaluation study and have reached agreement about what actions should be taken to improve the intervention or address other performance problems uncovered during the evaluation study. Of course, it is important to use this information to refine future analysis. It also is important, for purposes of continuous improvement, to apply the results of evaluation to an ongoing intervention if evaluators are conducting formative and concurrent evaluation (as they should be).

Implementing Step 10

This step loops back to the first step, prompting corrective action to improve interventions and supply the information desired by key stakeholders to make informed decisions and take informed actions.

During this step it is often worthwhile for WLP practitioners to assess the evaluation process itself. To that end, they might consider asking how well the evaluation study:

♦ Provided guidance for taking action to improve the intervention in the future

♦ Served to feed back information about results into the analysis process

♦ Served to stimulate action among key stakeholders

♦ Provided information that was useful to decision makers and stakeholders.

Use the Step 10 section in the worksheet in figure 4.1 to pose these and related questions about taking actions to improve the intervention and feeding back that information about results into the analysis process.

Vignette: At the end of one year, consultant Martin Mulderstein prepared to leave his client, the ABC Corporation. As he prepared to leave, he met with the steering committee and asked them to provide summary feedback to him about the evaluation process itself and about the intervention. He posed the questions suggested in this section and provided a summary report, as top managers of the organization had requested, to

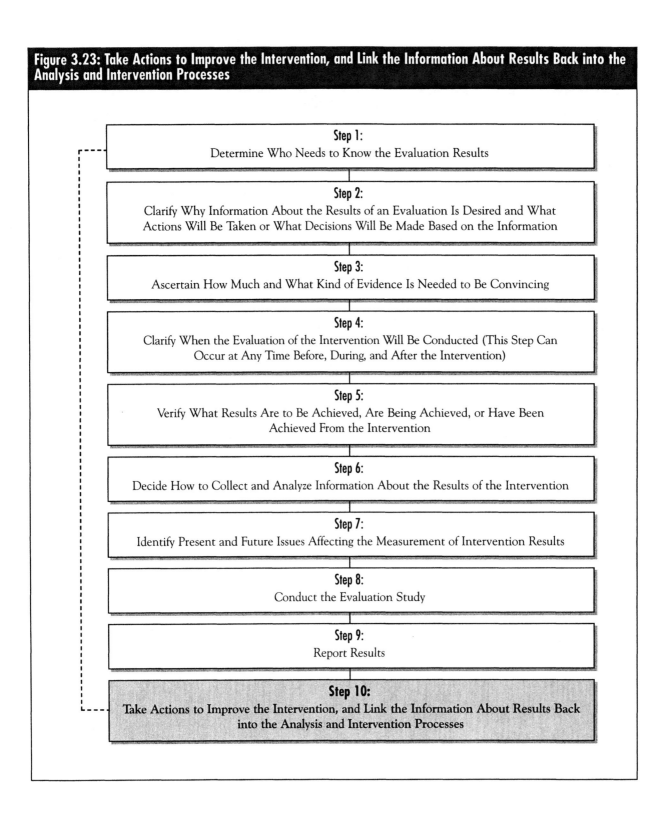

Figure 3.23: Take Actions to Improve the Intervention, and Link the Information About Results Back into the Analysis and Intervention Processes

Step 1:
Determine Who Needs to Know the Evaluation Results

Step 2:
Clarify Why Information About the Results of an Evaluation Is Desired and What Actions Will Be Taken or What Decisions Will Be Made Based on the Information

Step 3:
Ascertain How Much and What Kind of Evidence Is Needed to Be Convincing

Step 4:
Clarify When the Evaluation of the Intervention Will Be Conducted (This Step Can Occur at Any Time Before, During, and After the Intervention)

Step 5:
Verify What Results Are to Be Achieved, Are Being Achieved, or Have Been Achieved From the Intervention

Step 6:
Decide How to Collect and Analyze Information About the Results of the Intervention

Step 7:
Identify Present and Future Issues Affecting the Measurement of Intervention Results

Step 8:
Conduct the Evaluation Study

Step 9:
Report Results

Step 10:
Take Actions to Improve the Intervention, and Link the Information About Results Back into the Analysis and Intervention Processes

Introduction to the Tools Section

This section presents five tools:

1. **Worksheet to Guide Comprehensive Evaluation:** From the time you begin evaluation, use figure 4.1 to guide you through the evaluation process step by step.

2. **Questionnaire to Assess Participant Reactions:** Use figure 4.2 to collect the perceptions and reactions of participants to an intervention.

3. **Questionnaire to Assess Participant Change During an Intervention:** Use the questionnaire in figure 4.3 to examine participant change that results from an intervention.

4. **Worksheet to Assess the Financial Results of an Intervention:** Use figure 4.4 to examine the financial results of the intervention.

5. **Enclosed CD-ROM:** On the enclosed CD-ROM, you will find a comprehensive set of tools for assessing your current level of evaluation competencies, as well as a set of tools for calculating the return on investment (ROI) of various interventions. The competency assessment tools help you determine your current level of knowledge through two different means. You can take a post-test that is based on the content of the book. Your answers are automatically correlated to the evaluation competencies. The program will create a road map for your future development based on your knowledge gaps. You also can administer a 360-degree survey instrument that will give you a well-rounded view of your current skill level. Gather the insights of your peers, your direct reports, and your supervisor to gain a deeper appreciation of your strengths and needs for development.

Figure 4.1: Worksheet to Guide Comprehensive Evaluation

Directions: Use this tool to guide you from start to finish through a comprehensive evaluation. You do not have to use every question, and you may wish to add more questions when appropriate. However, the idea of this tool is to give you a template to guide your questioning and evaluative process.

Step 1: Determine Who Needs to Know the Evaluation Results

1	Who wants evaluation information? (Consider such stakeholder groups as WLP practitioners involved in analysis; WLP practitioners involved in evaluation; WLP practitioners enacting the role of manager; individuals or groups involved in an intervention; immediate supervisors of individuals or groups involved in an intervention; organizational policymakers and decision makers, such as top managers or stakeholders; the organization's customers or constituents; the organization's suppliers; the organization's distributors; family members of individuals participating in an intervention; government regulators, policymakers, and decision makers; union officials; members of the community; other specific groups, given the nature of the intervention.)
2	How much do they want to know?
3	When do they want to receive the information?
4	In what form do they want to receive the information?

Step 2: Clarify Why Information About the Results of an Evaluation Is Desired and What Actions Will Be Taken or What Decisions Will Be Made Based on the Information

5	Do decision makers want to know how much or how well intervention participants or other stakeholders will like, are liking, or have liked an intervention?
6	Do decision makers want to know how much or how well intervention participants or other stakeholders will change, are changing, or have changed as a direct result of an intervention?

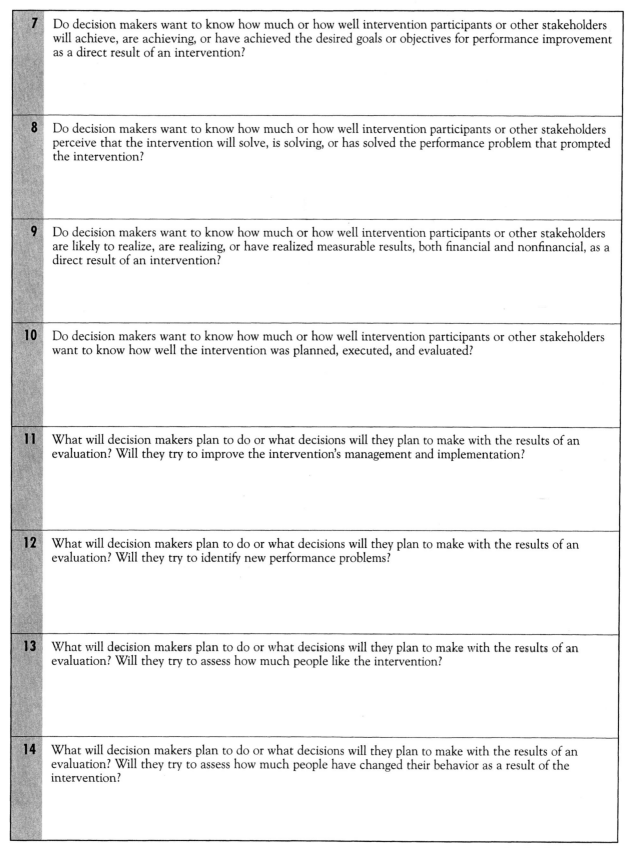

7	Do decision makers want to know how much or how well intervention participants or other stakeholders will achieve, are achieving, or have achieved the desired goals or objectives for performance improvement as a direct result of an intervention?
8	Do decision makers want to know how much or how well intervention participants or other stakeholders perceive that the intervention will solve, is solving, or has solved the performance problem that prompted the intervention?
9	Do decision makers want to know how much or how well intervention participants or other stakeholders are likely to realize, are realizing, or have realized measurable results, both financial and nonfinancial, as a direct result of an intervention?
10	Do decision makers want to know how much or how well intervention participants or other stakeholders want to know how well the intervention was planned, executed, and evaluated?
11	What will decision makers plan to do or what decisions will they plan to make with the results of an evaluation? Will they try to improve the intervention's management and implementation?
12	What will decision makers plan to do or what decisions will they plan to make with the results of an evaluation? Will they try to identify new performance problems?
13	What will decision makers plan to do or what decisions will they plan to make with the results of an evaluation? Will they try to assess how much people like the intervention?
14	What will decision makers plan to do or what decisions will they plan to make with the results of an evaluation? Will they try to assess how much people have changed their behavior as a result of the intervention?

(continued on next page)

	Figure 4.1: Worksheet to Guide Comprehensive Evaluation *(continued)*

	Step 2: Clarify Why Information About the Results of an Evaluation Is Desired and What Actions Will Be Taken or What Decisions Will Be Made Based on the Information *(continued)*
15	What will decision makers plan to do or what decisions will they plan to make with the results of an evaluation? Will they try to pinpoint what factors other than the intervention may have contributed to improvements during the intervention?
16	What will decision makers plan to do or what decisions will they plan to make with the results of an evaluation? Will they try to quantify how much the organization gained from the intervention in improved quantity of production, reduced production costs, improved production quality, reduced cycle time, improved customer service, or other measures?
17	What will decision makers plan to do or what decisions will they plan to make with the results of an evaluation? Will they try to justify the costs of the intervention based on the benefits received?
18	What will decision makers plan to do or what decisions will they plan to make with the results of an evaluation? Will they try to determine how well an intervention has helped to close performance gaps?
19	What other actions will be taken or decisions will be made based on the study results?
20	Collect background information about the external environment, the organization, and the intervention. Pose this question: Why do stakeholders want evaluation information, and what will they do with it once they have it?
21	What is happening with the intervention now?
22	Who is involved in implementing the intervention, and who is affected by it?
23	How has the intervention been linked to solving an important problem associated with the organization's business needs and strategic goals and objectives?

24	How much has the performance problem been costing the organization, and how much has the intervention cost?
25	When did the problem the intervention was designed to correct first appear or become noticeable?
26	Where has the problem the intervention was designed to correct been most evident? Are there geographical differences in which the intervention is being implemented more successfully or completely in some locales than in others?
27	What results have been achieved by the intervention?
28	What positive and negative side effects have resulted from the intervention that were not planned but were realized by the organization anyway?

Step 3: Ascertain How Much and What Kind of Evidence Is Needed to Be Convincing

29	What kind of evidence will be necessary to convince each stakeholder group? How much rigor and precision is needed, and how will that be judged?
30	How much should the stakeholders be actively involved in the design, data collection, and analysis of evaluation results to find the study's results persuasive?
31	How much evidence will be necessary to be convincing and credible to each stakeholder group?
32	In what form should the evidence be presented to be most useful to each stakeholder group?

(continued on next page)

Figure 4.1: Worksheet to Guide Comprehensive Evaluation *(continued)*

Step 4: Clarify When the Evaluation of the Intervention Will Be Conducted (This Step Can Occur At Any Time Before, During, and After the Intervention)

33	When should the evaluation be conducted?
34	Why should the evaluation be carried out at the time selected?
35	How should the evaluation study be carried out?
36	How much time, staff, money, and other resources are decision makers willing to provide to carry out the evaluation study at the time desired?

Step 5: Verify What Results Are to Be Achieved, Are Being Achieved, or Have Been Achieved from the Intervention

37	How clearly do people understand the performance expected of them in the intervention, and how much agreement exists among people that such performance is desirable?
38	How well can experienced performers recognize the situations in which they are expected to perform during the intervention (that is, identify performance cues)?
39	How often do people receive feedback on their performance during the intervention, how clear is the feedback they receive, and in what forms do they receive feedback?
40	What tools, equipment, and other resources are absolutely essential to performance during the intervention, and how many people have those available when they are needed?
41	How often do people confront decisions or situations for which they believe higher authority is needed for a decision during an intervention and how often is that access really necessary and available when needed?
42	How organized are the work processes of the intervention?

43	In what ways are people provided with incentives for performing during the intervention and rewarded for performing during the intervention? Do they see what's in it for them?
44	How much do people value the rewards they receive and believe that the performance required to achieve those rewards during the intervention is fair, capable of achievement, and will result in the promised rewards?
45	How willing are people to make bold (even risky) decisions to satisfy customers and achieve results through new, possibly untried methods during the intervention?
46	**Assessing desired results:** What issues or trends in the work environment call for new action? Where are competitive conditions headed, and why?
47	**Assessing desired results:** What are the performance differences between the best-performing organizations in the industry, and how does their performance (as measured by return on equity or numerous other measures) compare to that of the organization in which the analysis is conducted?
48	**Assessing desired results:** What is the difference between the highest-performing and the lowest-performing work units and individuals? What accounts for those differences?
49	**Assessing desired results:** How should the organization provide guidance to performers about what is expected of them, and how should disagreements be resolved?
50	**Assessing desired results:** What key business issues are affecting this organization? Which ones are most important, and why are they most important?
51	**Assessing desired results:** How profitable is the organization now? How profitable should it be in the future? What are the goals for profitability?
52	**Assessing desired results:** What return on investment (ROI) and return on equity (ROE) is the organization realizing now? What are its goals in those areas? (If it is a large organization, what business units are realizing the greatest ROI and ROE, and why exactly are they more successful than others?)

(continued on next page)

	Figure 4.1: Worksheet to Guide Comprehensive Evaluation *(continued)*
	Step 5: Verify What Results Are to Be Achieved, Are Being Achieved, or Have Been Achieved From the Intervention *(continued)*
53	**Assessing desired results:** What is the organization's targeted market share? How was that target established, and how realistic is it?
54	**Assessing desired results:** What are the targets for quality? What error rates have been targeted? How realistic are those targets, and have they ever been achieved?
55	**Assessing desired results:** What are the targets for customer satisfaction? How have those been identified, measured, and tracked? What feedback is given about customer satisfaction to performers, and how much should they be receiving?
56	**About an intervention:** What should be happening, and what results or outcomes are desired?
57	**About an intervention:** Who should be involved to make that happen?
58	**About an intervention:** How will the realization of the intervention's goal help meet the organization's business needs and achieve strategic goals and objectives?
59	**About an intervention:** When are these desired results to be achieved? Over what time span?
60	**About an intervention:** What interim goals or milestones could be achieved over time toward realization of the ultimate goal?
61	**About an intervention:** What does the "optimal state" look like? What will be happening when it is achieved? What results will be obtained?
62	**About an intervention:** What steps already have been taken to create a vision or spell out the desirable results to be achieved, and what level of agreement among decision makers has been reached on those?

	Step 6: Decide How to Collect and Analyze Information About the Results of the Intervention
63	When should information be collected about the results of the intervention?
64	How should that information be collected? What methods or data collection approaches should be used, and what systematic approach can help to guide the data collection process?
65	How should the data be analyzed, and why are those analytical methods most appropriate for the stakeholders targeted to receive the data?

	Step 7: Identify Present and Future Issues Affecting the Measurement of Intervention Results
66	**Classify the external environment into sectors—economic conditions:** What changes are expected in the business cycle, and how might those influence the results obtained by an intervention?
67	**Classify the external environment into sectors—political conditions:** What changes are expected in political conditions, and how might those influence the results obtained by an intervention?
68	**Classify the external environment into sectors—legal/regulatory conditions:** What changes are expected in legal and regulatory conditions, and how might those influence the results obtained by an intervention?
69	**Classify the external environment into sectors—social conditions:** What changes are expected in social conditions, and how might those influence the results obtained by an intervention?
70	**Classify the external environment into sectors—market conditions:** What changes are expected in market conditions, and how might those influence the results achieved by an intervention?
71	**Classify the external environment into sectors—competitors inside the industry:** What changes are expected from competitors inside the industry, and how might those influence the results obtained by an intervention?
72	**Classify the external environment into sectors—competitors outside the industry:** What changes are expected from competitors outside the industry, and how might those influence the results obtained by an intervention?

(continued on next page)

Figure 4.1: Worksheet to Guide Comprehensive Evaluation *(continued)*

Step 7: Identify Present and Future Issues Affecting the Measurement of Intervention Results *(continued)*

73	**Classify the external environment into sectors—suppliers:** What changes are expected from suppliers, and how might those influence the results obtained by an intervention?
74	**Classify the external environment into sectors—distributors:** What changes are expected from distributors, and how might those influence the results obtained by an intervention?
75	**Classify the external environment into sectors—geographic issues:** What changes are expected with the placement of key materials, suppliers, distributors, or customers, and how might those influence the results obtained by an intervention?
76	**Classify the external environment into sectors—technology:** What changes are expected in technology, and how might those influence the results obtained by an intervention?
77	**Consider an alternative approach to classifying the external environment:** What trends outside the organization have affected the intervention most as it was implemented?
78	**Consider an alternative approach to classifying the external environment:** What trends outside the organization are likely to affect the intervention in the future?
79	**Consider an alternative approach to classifying the external environment:** How have factual or perceived results of the intervention changed over time, and how might those results change in the future?
80	**Consider an alternative approach to classifying the external environment:** How might these changes in conditions outside the intervention affect the results of the intervention as measured by how much stakeholders like it, have seen change resulting from it, or realized measurable gains from it?
81	**Consider an alternative approach to classifying the external environment—time horizon:** How far into the future will the scanning project? How far into the future do stakeholders wish to assess the financial or nonfinancial value of an intervention?

82	**Consider an alternative approach to classifying the external environment. Examine the external environmental sectors for expected changes over the time horizon chosen:** What changes have occurred outside the organization as the intervention was implemented, and what changes are expected to occur in the future that may influence the results obtained from the intervention? What is the best guess about the impact of an intervention over the time horizon that has been chosen?
83	**Consider an alternative approach to classifying the external environment:** What will be the likely measurable effects of environmental changes on the intervention?

Step 8: Conduct the Evaluation Study

84	How well does the project plan work in practice as it is implemented?
85	During the evaluation study, is it apparent that insufficient resources were applied to the study? If so, how is this problem solved?
86	During the evaluation study, did key stakeholders change? Was the evaluation study design reconsidered in light of possible new information requirements of new stakeholders?
87	During the evaluation study, were issues discovered that involved the intervention that were unknown at the time the evaluation study was planned? How were those issues handled?
88	Was there difficulty in collecting the desired information as the evaluation study was conducted? If so, how was that issue addressed?

Step 9: Report Results

89	How well was the report prepared?
90	How well does the report minimize the time requirements of the listener or reader?
91	How well does the report provide the information required by the key stakeholders?

(continued on next page)

Figure 4.1: Worksheet to Guide Comprehensive Evaluation *(continued)*

Step 9: Report Results *(continued)*

92	How well does the report answer this question: What was the intervention, and what performance problem was it intended to solve?
93	How well does the report answer this question: What was happening before the intervention was implemented, and what evidence existed to indicate the nature, cost, and scope of the performance problem?
94	How well does the report answer this question: How was the intervention carried out, by whom, at what locations, using what methods, and over what time?
95	How well does the report answer this question: What stakeholders wanted to receive information about the results of the intervention, what kind of information did they want to receive, and how were they polled for their preferences?
96	How well does the report answer this question: How was the evaluation study carried out, by whom, at what locations, using what methods, and over what time?
97	How well does the report answer this question: What was happening after the intervention was implemented, and what evidence existed to indicate the nature, benefits received, and scope of the intervention?
98	How well does the report answer this question: What problems arose during the evaluation study, and how were they addressed?
99	How well does the report answer this question: What was the measurable difference between the performance problem as it existed before the intervention and its current status after the intervention?
100	How well does the report answer this question: What factors outside the control of evaluators may have influenced the outcomes of the evaluation study, and how much influence did they have over the results?
101	How well does the report answer this question: What future factors might affect future benefits received from the intervention?

102	How well does the report answer this question: What recommendations could be made for improving the intervention in the future?

Step 10: Take Actions to Improve the Intervention and Link the Information About Results Back into the Analysis and Intervention Processes	
103	How well did the evaluation study provide guidance for taking action to improve the intervention in the future?
104	How well the did the evaluation study serve to link information about results back into the analysis process?
105	How well did the evaluation study serve to stimulate action among key stakeholders?
106	How well did the evaluation study provide information that was useful to decision makers and stakeholders?

Figure 4.2: Questionnaire to Assess Participant Reactions

Directions for Use by WLP Practitioners: Participant reactions are sometimes measured at the end of training by such means as "smile sheets" or reaction surveys provided at the end of training. The same basic approach may be used with *any* intervention. To do that, simply modify an existing participant reaction questionnaire to assess participant reactions about a specific intervention. Be clear which intervention is being evaluated! Administer this survey by mail, email, fax—or else use these questions to guide a focus group of participants.

Questionnaire to Assess Participant Reactions

Directions: Use this questionnaire to provide your reactions and feedback about *[insert a brief description of the intervention]*. There are no "right" or "wrong" answers in any absolute sense. Mark your reactions as soon as possible, since your first reaction is likely to be most accurate. When you finish, return your completed survey questionnaire to *[individual]* at *[address]* by *[date]*. Thank you for your cooperation!

Provide your responses in the left column. Use the following scale to rate your attitudes, perceptions, and feelings about the intervention:

Strongly Agree	Agree	Slightly Agree	Neutral	Slightly Disagree	Disagree	Strongly Disagree
7	6	5	4	3	2	1

Intervention Purpose, Objectives, Plan

1. The purpose of the intervention was clear.

2. The need for the intervention was apparent to me, and I understood the business need or problem that prompted it.

3. The objectives guiding the intervention were clear.

4. The plan to guide the intervention was clear.

5. The purpose, objectives, and plan guiding the intervention were well-communicated.

Intervention Materials and Methods

6. The materials used in the intervention—including Websites, procedure manuals, or other documents that were made available to help people perform—were clear and useful to me.

7. The materials used in the intervention were able to guide people to new performance that seemed to be consistent with the intervention's requirements and objectives.

8. The methods used in the intervention—such as training, meetings, and other approaches to build people's knowledge about it and keep it on track—were clear and useful to me.

9. The methods used in the intervention were able to guide people to new performance.

Intervention Implementation Approaches

☐   10. Managers, supervisors, and others supported and encouraged my participation in the intervention.

☐   11. Managers, supervisors, and others set a positive example to demonstrate their commitment to the intervention.

☐   12. Managers, supervisors, and others provided sufficient resources (time and money) to implement the intervention successfully.

☐   13. I felt encouraged to voice my views about the intervention as it was being implemented so that it would yield the results desired.

☐   14. I had ample opportunity to voice my views about the intervention as it was being implemented.

Intervention Results

☐   15. Overall, I liked the intervention.

☐   16. Overall, I felt the intervention led people to change their behavior.

☐   17. Overall, I felt that the intervention solved the problem it was intended to solve.

18. What did you feel was done particularly well in this intervention? Why did you feel that way?

19. What do you feel could have been improved in this intervention? Why do you feel that way?

20. What other remarks do you have to make about this intervention?

Thank you for your cooperation!

(Please return this completed survey to [individual] at [address] by [date].)

Figure 4.3: Questionnaire to Assess Participant Change During an Intervention

Directions for Use by WLP Practitioners: Participant change resulting from an intervention is sometimes measured at the end of training by such means as follow-up survey questionnaires to participants and their immediate supervisors some time after they attended the training. You may use the same basic approach with *any* intervention to gather perceptions about on-the-job change occurring during the intervention. Administer the survey that follows to participants in the intervention by mail, email, fax—or use these questions to guide a focus group meeting of participants and their immediate supervisors. (You also could modify this survey to collect perceptions from immediate supervisors of the participants in an intervention to triangulate—or double-check—the results.

Questionnaire to Assess Participant Change Resulting from an Intervention

Directions: Use this questionnaire to provide your reactions and feedback about the on-the-job change(s) you have made during *[insert a brief description of the intervention]*. There are no "right" or "wrong" answers in any absolute sense. Mark your reactions as soon as possible, since your first reaction is likely to be most accurate. When you finish, return your completed survey questionnaire to *[individual]* at *[address]* by *[date]*. Thank you for your cooperation!

Provide your responses in the left column. Use the following scale to rate your attitudes, perceptions, and feelings about how much on-the-job change has occurred during the intervention:

Strongly Agree	Agree	Slightly Agree	Neutral	Slightly Disagree	Disagree	Strongly Disagree
7	6	5	4	3	2	1

My Views About the Intervention

1. I understand the purpose of the intervention.

2. I understand the business need for this intervention.

3. I understand what behavior changes I need to make on the job to make the intervention successful.

4. I feel that I possess adequate knowledge, skills, and abilities to make necessary changes on the job in order to help implement the intervention successfully.

5. I feel that I have been provided with the resources that I need to make necessary changes on the job to help implement the intervention successfully.

6. I believe my immediate supervisor has encouraged me to change my on-the-job behavior in ways that will help implement the intervention.

On-The-Job Behavior Change

☐ 7. I believe that I have been successful in changing my on-the-job behavior in ways that will help to implement the intervention. If you agree with this statement, describe briefly below *how you have changed and how much you have changed your own the job behavior.*

Description of on-the-job behavior change.

☐ 8. Some conditions in the work environment may have made it more difficult to change your on-the-job behavior in ways that will help implement the intervention. If you agree with this statement, describe briefly below *what those conditions are.*

Description of conditions in the work environment that have made it difficult to change on-the-job behavior:

☐ 9. Some conditions in the work environment may have made it easier to change your on-the-job behavior in ways that will help implement the intervention. If you agree with this statement, describe briefly below *what those conditions are.*

Description of conditions in the work environment that have made it easier to change on-the-job behavior:

Intervention Results

☐ 10. I believe that the organization has gained more than it has spent on the intervention. If you agree with this statement, describe briefly below *how you believe the organization has gained from the intervention and how that gain is best or most appropriately measured in dollar terms.*

Key benefits of the intervention:

Thank you for your cooperation!

(Please return this completed survey to [individual] at [address] by [date].)

Figure 4.4: Worksheet to Assess the Financial Results of an Intervention

Directions for Use by WLP Practitioners: Decision makers often question WLP practitioners about the financial results of an intervention. They would like to know the answer to this question: What financial benefit was gained from the intervention? While that question is sometimes best asked before an investment decision is made for an intervention, it is sometimes necessary to do an after-the-fact estimate of financial results. Many methods and approaches have been suggested to handle this issue.

Administer the worksheet below to key decision makers after the intervention has been implemented. Use it simply to gather their perceptions about the financial results obtained from the intervention. You also may modify the worksheet to forecast (before an intervention is implemented) the likely costs and benefits resulting from it.

Worksheet to Assess the Financial Results of an Intervention

Directions: Use this worksheet to assess the financial results of an intervention.

Part I: Demographic Information

Interviewer's Name _____   Today's Date _____

Respondent's Name _____   Respondent's Title/Department _____

Respondent's Address _____

Respondent's Phone/fax _____

Part II. Before the Intervention

1. What was the performance problem that the intervention was intended to solve?

Problem	Likely Causes of the Problem
Describe the problem:	*List likely cause(s):*

Part II: Cost of the Problem

2. What is the problem costing the organization before the intervention began? Please check the following ways the problem could be costing the organization and estimate how much it is or was costing the organization *annually*.

Possible Costs of the Problem	Is The Problem Costing the Organization in this Area?		How much would you estimate the problem is costing the organization annually?
	Yes	No	
Decreased competitiveness			
Decreased profitability			
Decreased quality			
Decreased customer service			
Decreased production			
Decreased sales			
Increased waste			
Increased cycle time			
Increased absenteeism			
Increased turnover			
Increased accident rates			
Other			
Total *(Estimate total cost of the problem annually)*			$

(continued on next page)

Part III: Cost of the Intervention

3. What will/has the intervention cost to solve the problem? Please estimate the annual budget to solve the problem below.

Possible Budget Category	Is This Budget Category Applicable to this Project		How much would you estimate it will cost annually to solve the problem by using intervention?
	Yes	No	
Analyzing the problem			
Salaries and wages			
Travel costs			
Mail/phone/fax			
Other expenses			
Designing and developing the intervention *(preparing materials and methods)*			
Salaries and wages			
Travel costs			
Mail/phone/fax			
Other expenses			
Implementing the intervention			
Salaries and wages			
Travel costs			
Mail/phone/fax			
Other expense (specify)			

Possible Budget Category	Is This Budget Category Applicable to this Project		How much would you estimate it will cost annually to solve the problem by using intervention?
	Yes	No	
Evaluating *(including cost of collecting information)*			
Salaries and wages			
Travel costs			
Mail/phone/fax			
Other expenses			

Total *(Estimate total cost of the training annually)* $

Part IV: Cost of Problem Minus Cost of the Intervention

4. What will be the estimated annual cost of the problem minus the estimated annual cost of the intervention? *Please estimate the difference below:*

Estimated Annual Cost of the Problem	Minus	Estimated Annual Cost of the Intervention	Difference
$	—	$	$

Source: Rothwell. *Creating, Measuring & Documenting Service Impact: A Capacity Building Resource: Rationales, Models, Activities, Techniques, Instruments* (pp. 89-93.) Columbus, OH: EnterpriseOhio Network, 1998.

This section addresses three key issues:

1. Why is it important to master the role of evaluator and the competencies associated with it?
2. How does it feel to perform the role of evaluator?
3. What should you do next?

Why Is It Important to Master the Role of Evaluator and the Competencies Associated With It?

Evaluation is the last step in the HPI Process Model, but the role of evaluator is by no means the least important role. Without it, WLP practitioners cannot determine the impact of an intervention. In turn, a practitioner who cannot ascertain the value of an intervention will not be positioned to prove the worth of the intervention to stakeholders, ensure continuous improvement of the intervention, or demonstrate that the intervention solved the performance problem that it was intended to solve.

Interventions can have a multitude of possible effects (both planned and unplanned), just as performance problems can have a multitude of possible causes. You may find it as difficult to demonstrate the full impact of an intervention—including its positive side effects—as isolating the cause(s) of a performance problem. But unless you are willing to settle for no evaluation, you will have to undertake the challenge of evaluation.

The key to evaluation lies in determining who wants to know the results of the evaluation study, why they want to know, and what they plan to do with that information. It is a mistake to believe you can demonstrate conclusively the full impact of an intervention successfully to all stakeholders in every

case. Your goal should be to provide clear and convincing evidence that the intervention has been successful based on the information requirements of the key stakeholder(s).

How Does It Feel to Perform the Role of Evaluator?

Performing the role of evaluator can feel a bit like playing detective. Like good detectives, competent evaluators remain objective. They are dedicated to uncovering the impact of interventions. Often the people who come to the evaluator purportedly to seek information about results (top managers, for instance) already have formed opinions about what they believe. They sometimes can be impatient to show results and are essentially looking to you for confirmation of the intervention's value. To be effective, the evaluator must seek to satisfy the information requirements of key stakeholders.

What Should You Do Next?

The Evaluator is the second of several self-study job aids introduced in *ASTD Models for Workplace Learning and Performance* (1999). Other volumes focus on such other possible WLP roles as manager, analyst, intervention selector, intervention designer and developer, intervention implementor, and change leader. Use all the job aids to help build your competencies.

You might find it useful as well to refer to the CD-ROM that accompanies this volume and the volume on the analyst's role. It can help you assess what you have learned from the text, assess your present and future competencies, and identify actions you can take to help build them.

BIBLIOGRAPHY

Addicott, P. (1991). ROI model gives training new respected cost justification. *Training Director's Forum Newsletter, 7*(6), 4–5.

Alliger, G., and Janak, E. (1989). Kirkpatrick's levels of training criteria: Thirty years later. *Personnel Psychology, 42*(2), 331–342.

Anderson, P. (1991). Matrix helps designers balance program time and cost. *Training Directors Forum Newsletter, 7*(12), 5.

A rating scale for adult learning. *Training, 27*(2), 63–64. Presents an evaluation form based on principles of adult learning theory.

Arvey, R., Maxwell, S., and Salas, E. (1992). The relative power of training evaluation designs under different cost configurations. *Journal of Applied Psychology, 77*(2), 155–160.

Bachman, L. (1987). Pilot your program for success. *Training and Development Journal, 41*(5), 96–97.

Bates, R. (1999). Measuring performance improvement. In R. Torrace (Ed.), *Performance improvement theory and practice*. San Francisco: Berrett-Koehler.

Biner, P. (1993). The development of an instrument to measure student attitudes toward televised courses. *American Journal of Distance Education, 7*(1), 62–73.

Blomberg, R. (1989). Cost-benefit analysis of employee training: A literature review. *Adult Education Quarterly, 39*(2), 89–98.

Bohan, G., and Horney, N. (1991). Pinpointing the real cost of quality in a service company. *National Productivity Review, 10*(3), 309–317.

Boudreau, J.W., and Ramstad, P.M. (1996). *Measuring intellectual capital: Learning from financial history.* Ithaca, NY: Cornell University Center for Advanced Human Resource Studies.

Brauchle, P. (1992). Costing out the value of training. *Technical & Skills Training, 3*(4), 35–40.

Brethower, D. (1993). Strategic improvement of workplace competence II: The economics of competence. *Performance Improvement Quarterly, 6*(2), 29–42.

Brinkerhoff, R. (1987). *Achieving results from training.* San Francisco: Jossey-Bass.

Broad, M., and Newstrom, J. (1992). *Transfer of training: Action-packed strategies to ensure high payoff from training investments.* Reading, MA: Addison-Wesley.

Bushnell, D. (1990). Input, process, output: A model for evaluating training. *Training and Development Journal, 44*(3), 41–43.

Campion, M., and McClelland, C. (1993). Follow-up and extension of the interdisciplinary costs and benefits of enlarged jobs. *Journal of Applied Psychology, 78*(3), 339–351.

Carnevale, A., and Schulz, E. (1990). Return on investment: Accounting for training. *Training and Development 44*(7), s1–32.

Cascio, W.F. (1987). *Costing human resources: The financial impact of behavior in organizations.* Boston: PAWS-Kent Publishing.

Chernick, J. (1992). Keeping your pilots on course. *Training and Development, 46*(4), 69–73.

Clements, J.C., and Josiam, B.M. (1995). Training: Quantifying the financial benefits. *International Journal of Contemporary Hospitality Management, 1*(1), 10–15.

Coffman, L. (1990). Involving managers in training evaluation. *Training and Development Journal, 44*(6), 77–80.

Crook, B. (1990). Benchmarking with respected companies highlights gaps in the training function. *Training Directors Forum Newsletter, 6*(7), 4–5.

Cullen, G., Sawzin, S., Sisson, G.R., and Swanson, R.A. (1978). Cost effectiveness: A model for assessing the training investment. *Training and Development Journal, 32*(1), 24–29

Cullen, G., Sawzin. S., Sisson, G.R., and Swanson, R.A. (1976). Training, what's it worth? *Training and Development Journal, 30*(8), 12–20.

Davidove, E. (1993). Evaluating the return on investment in training. *Performance and Instruction, 32*(1), 1–8.

Davidove, E., and Schroeder, P. (1992). Demonstrating ROI of training. *Training and Development, 46*(8), 70–71.

Demeuse, K.P., and Liebowitz, S.J. (1981). An empirical analysis of team building sesearch. *Group and organizational skills, 6*(3), 357–378.

Deming, B. (1982). *Evaluating job-related training.* Alexandria, VA: ASTD.

Denova, C. (1979). *Test construction for training evaluation.* New York: Van Nostrand Reinhold.

Dennis, V. (1992). The problem of split budget responsibility. *CBT Directions, 5*(1), 6–9.

Dixon, N. (1990). The relationship between trainee responses on participant reaction forms and posttest scores. *Human Resource Development Quarterly, 1*(2), 129–137.

Erkut, S. and Fields, J. (1987). Focus groups to the rescue. *Training and Development Journal, 41*(10), 74–76.

Filipczak, B. (1992). The business of training at NCR. *Training, 29*(2), 55–60.

Fisk, C. (Ed.). (1991). *ASTD trainer's toolkit: Evaluation instruments.* Alexandria, VA: ASTD. Contains 25 sample instruments.

Fitz-Enz, J. (1990). *Human value management.* San Francisco: Jossey-Bass.

Flamholtz, E.G. (1985). *Human resource accounting.* San Francisco, CA: Jossey-Bass.

Ford, D. (1993). Benchmarking HRD. *Training and Development, 47*(6), 36–41.

Garavaglia, P. (1993). How to ensure transfer of training. *Training and Development, 47*(10), 63–68.

Geroy, G.D., and Swanson, R.A. (1984). Forecasting training costs and benefits in industry. *Journal of Epsilon Pi Tau, 10*(2), 15–19.

Gillies, D. (1991). Fine-tuning nurse management education through formative evaluation. *Journal of Continuing Education in the Health Professions, 11*(3), 229–242.

Gordon, J. (1991). Measuring the 'goodness' of training. *Training, 28*(8), 19–25.

Harris, D., and Bell, C. (1986). *Evaluating and assessing for learning.* London: Kogan Page.

Harrison, P. (1991). Development of a distance education assessment instrument. *Educational Technology Research and Development, 39*(4), 65–77.

Hartz, R., Niemiec, R., and Walberg, H. (1993). The impact of management education. *Performance Improvement Quarterly, 6*(1), 67–76.

Hassett, J. (1992). Predicting the costs of training. *Training and Development, 46*(11), 40–44.

Hassett, J. (1992). Simplifying ROI. *Training, 29*(9), 53–57.

Hawley, J. (1991). A practical methodology for determining cost-effective instructional programs. *Performance & Instruction, 30*(5), 17–23.

Head, G.E. (1985). *Training cost analysis.* Washington, D.C.: Marlin Press.

Heideman, J. (1993). The team approach to formative evaluation. *Technical & Skills Training, 4*(3), 9–12.

Hendricks, K.B., and Singhal, V.R. (1995). *Does implementing an effective TQM program actually improve operating performance? Empirical evidence from firms that have won quality awards.* Williamsburg, VA: School of Business, College of William and Mary.

Holton, E.F. (1996). The flawed four-level evaluation model. *Human Resource Development Quarterly, 7*(1), 5–21.

Hornbeck, D., and Salamon, L. (1991). *Human capital and America's future: An economic strategy for the 90's.* Baltimore: Johns Hopkins Press.

Hronec, S.M. (1993). *Vital signs: Using quality, time, and cost performance measurements to chart your company's future.* New York: AMACOM.

Ives, B., and Forman, D. (1991). Winning over the bean counters. *CBT Directions, 4*(6), 10–18.

Jacobs, R., Jones, M., and Neil, S. (1992). A case study in forecasting the financial benefits of unstructured and structured on-the-job training. *Human Resource Development Quarterly, 3*(2),133–139.

Jones, J. (1990). Don't smile about smile sheets. *Training and Development Journal, 44*(12), 19–21.

Kaufman, R., and Kaufman, J. (1992). What should high risk operations evaluate relative to safety and safety training? *Performance Improvement Quarterly, 5*(3), 16–25.

Kearsley, G. (1982). *Costs, benefits, productivity in training systems.* Reading, MA: Addison-Wesley Publishing.

Kirkpatrick, D.L. (1994). *Evaluating training programs: The four levels.* San Francisco: Berrett-Koehler.

Kolb, K. (1991). Meaningful methods: Evaluation without the crunch. *Journal of Experiential Education, 14*(1), 40–44.

Kraiger, K., Ford, J., and Salas, E. (1993). Application of cognitive, skill-based, and affective theories of learning outcomes to new methods of training evaluation. *Journal of Applied Psychology, 78*(2), 311–328.

Kropp, R. (1991). Some reasons for the development of a new model for evaluating training programs. *Journal of Research in Learning in the Workplace, 1*(1), 67–100.

Lamos, J., Villachica, S., and Stone, D. (1991). Is your CBT worthwhile? *CBT Directions, 4*(9), 16–21.

Lee, W., and Roadman, K. (1990). *Ensuring instructional soundness through sound evaluation.* Columbus, OH: Association for the Development of Computer-Based Instructional Systems. ERIC Document 333862.

McLagan, P. (1989). *Models for HRD practice* (4 volumes). Alexandria, VA: ASTD.

McLinden, D., and Cook, S. (1990). Getting more information out of reactions to training: Using the technique of paired comparisons. *Performance & Instruction, 29*(5), 24–29.

Marelli, A. (1993). Determining training costs, benefits, and results. *Technical & Skills Training, 4*(7), 35–40.

Marelli, A. (1993). Ten evaluation instruments for technical training. *Technical & Skills Training, 4*(5), 7–14.

Marshall, V., and Schriver, R. (1994). Using evaluation to improve performance. *Technical & Skills Training, 5*(1), 6–9.

Merlo, N. (1988). Subjective ROI. *Training and Development Journal, 42*(11), 63–66.

Mincer, J. (1962). On-the-job training: Costs, returns, and some implications. *Journal of Political Economy, 52*(5), part 2, 50–79.

Minton-Eversole, T. (1993). The training evaluation process. *Training & Development, 47*(1), 78.

Mosier, N. (1990). Financial analysis methods and their application to employee training. *Human Resource Development Quarterly, 1*(1), 45–71.

Nicholas, S., and Langseth, R.W. (1982). The comparative impact of organization development interventions on hard criteria measures. *Academy of Management Review, 1*(2), 531–542.

O'Donnell, J. (1988). Focus groups: A habit-forming evaluating technique. *Training and Development Journal, 42*(7), 71–73.

Ostroff, C. (1991). Training effectiveness measures and scoring schemes: A comparison. *Personnel Psychology, 44*(2) 353–374.

Patton, M. (1987). *Creative evaluation.* Beverly Hills, CA: Sage Publications.

Phillips, J. (1994). *In action: Measuring return on investment.* Alexandria, VA: ASTD.

Phillips, J. (1991). *Handbook of training evaluation and measurement methods* (second edition). Houston, TX: Gulf Publishing.

Pine, J., and Tingley, J. (1993). ROI of soft-skills training. *Training, 30*(2), 55–60.

Rae, L. (1991). *How to measure training effectiveness.* Brookfield, VT: Gower Publishing.

Resource guide: Evaluation. (1994). Alexandria, VA: ASTD.

Romanelli, E., and Tushman, M.L. (1994). Organizational transformation as punctuated equilibrium: An empirical test. *Academy of Management Journal, 37*(5), 1141–1166.

Rosentreter, G.E. (1979). Economic evaluation of a training program. In R. O. Peterson (Ed.), *Studies in training and development: Research papers from the 1978 ASTD national conference.* Madison, WI: ASTD.

Rothwell, W. (Ed.). (1998a). *Creating, measuring & documenting service impact: A capacity building resource: Rationales, models, activities, techniques, instruments.* Columbus, OH: EnterpriseOhio Network.

Rothwell, W. (1998b). Standards. In W. Rothwell (Ed.), *Creating, measuring & documenting service impact: A capacity building resource: Rationales, models, activities, techniques, instruments.* Columbus, OH: EnterpriseOhio Network.

Rothwell, W. (1998c). A model for measuring service impact. In W. Rothwell (Ed.), *Creating, measuring & documenting service impact: A capacity building resource: Rationales, models, activities, techniques, instruments.* Columbus, OH: EnterpriseOhio Network.

Rothwell, W. (1998d). Frequently-asked questions about the process. In W. Rothwell (Ed.), *Creating, measuring & documenting service impact: A capacity building resource: Rationales, models, activities, techniques, instruments.* Columbus, OH: EnterpriseOhio Network.

Rothwell, W. (1998e). An approach to forecasting return on investments. In W. Rothwell (Ed.), *Creating, measuring & documenting service impact: A capacity building resource: Rationales, models, activities, techniques, instruments.* Columbus, OH: EnterpriseOhio Network.

Rothwell, W. (1998f). A worksheet for forecasting financial benefits of training. In W. Rothwell (Ed.), *Creating, measuring & documenting service impact: A capacity building resource: Rationales, models, activities, techniques, instruments.* Columbus, OH: EnterpriseOhio Network.

Rothwell, W. (1998g). Composite sample proposal. In W. Rothwell (Ed.), *Creating, measuring & documenting service impact: A capacity building resource: Rationales, models, activities, techniques, instruments.* Columbus, OH: EnterpriseOhio Network.

Rothwell, W. (1998h). An overview of techniques to use to measure training/interventions during the interventions. In W. Rothwell (Ed.), *Creating, measuring & documenting service impact: A capacity building resource: Rationales, models, activities, techniques, instruments.* Columbus, OH: EnterpriseOhio Network.

Rothwell, W. (1998i). The transfer of learning assessment instrument. In W. Rothwell (Ed.), *Creating, measuring & documenting service impact: A capacity building resource: Rationales, models, activities, techniques, instruments.* Columbus, OH: EnterpriseOhio Network.

Rothwell, W. (1998j). Financial measurement interview guide. In W. Rothwell (Ed.), *Creating, measuring & documenting service impact: A capacity building resource: Rationales, models, activities, techniques, instruments.* Columbus, OH: EnterpriseOhio Network.

Rothwell, W. (1998k). The success case method. In W. Rothwell (Ed.), *Creating, measuring & documenting service impact: A capacity building resource: Rationales, models, activities, techniques, instruments.* Columbus, OH: EnterpriseOhio Network.

Rothwell, W. (1994). *Effective succession planning: Ensuring leadership continuity and building talent from within.* New York: AMACOM.

Rothwell, W., Hohne, C., and King, S. (2000). *Human performance improvement: Building practitioner competence (Improving Human Performance Series).* Houston, TX: Gulf Publishing.

Rothwell, W., and Kazanas, H. (1998). *Mastering the instructional design process: A systematic approach* (second edition). San Francisco: Jossey-Bass.

Rothwell, W., and Kazanas, H. (1994). *Human resource development: A strategic approach* (revised edition). Amherst, MA: Human Resource Development Press.

Rothwell, W., and Kazanas, H. (1993). Developing management employees to cope with the moving target effect. *Performance and Instruction, 32*(8), 1–5.

Rothwell, W., and Lindholm, J. (1999). Competency identification, modeling and assessment in the USA. *International Journal of Training and Development, 3*(2), 90–105.

Rothwell, W., Prescott, R., and Taylor, M. (1998). *Strategic human resource leader.* Palo Alto, CA: Davies-Black.

Rothwell, W., Sanders, E., and Soper, J. (1999). *ASTD models for workplace learning and performance: Roles, competencies, and outputs.* Alexandria, VA: ASTD.

Rothwell, W., and Sredl, H. (2000). *The ASTD reference guide to workplace learning and performance: Present and future roles and competencies* (third edition, 2 volumes). Amherst, MA: Human Resource Development Press.

Russell, J., and Blake, B. (1988). Formative and summative evaluation of instructional products and learners. *Educational Technology, 28*(9), 22–28.

Sebrell, W. (1990). Calculating training quality. *Computerworld, 24*(2), 120.

Schmidt, F.L., Hunter, J.E., McKenzie, R.C., and Muldrow, T.W. (1979). Impact of valid selection procedures on work-force productivity. *Journal of Applied Psychology, 64,* 609–626.

Schmidt, F.L., Hunter, J.E., Outerbridge, A.N., and Tratmer, M.H. (1986). The economic impact of job selection methods on size, productivity, and payroll costs of the federal work force: An empirically-based demonstration. *Personnel Psychology, 39,* 1–30.

Schmidt, F.L., Hunter, J.E, and Pearlman, K. (1982). Assessing the economic impact of personnel programs on work-force productivity. *Personnel Psychology, 35,* 335–347.

Shelton, S. and Alliger, G. (1993). Who's afraid of level 4 evaluation?: A practical approach. *Training & Development, 47*(6), 43–46.

Sleezer, C. (Ed.). (1989). *Improving human resource development through measurement.* Alexandria, VA: ASTD.

Sleezer, C., Cipicchio, D., and Pitonyak, D. (1992). Customizing and implementing training evaluation. *Performance Improvement Quarterly, 5*(4), 55–75.

Smith, M., and Brandenburg, D. (1991). Summative evaluation. *Performance Improvement Quarterly, 4*(2), 35–58.

Smith, J., and Merchant, S. (1990). Using competency exams for evaluating training. *Training and Development Journal, 44*(8), 65–71.

Spencer, L.M., Jr. (1986). *Calculating human resource costs and benefits.* New York: Wiley Publishing.

Steps in human performance analysis. (1996). *Training & Development, 50*(12), 48.

Stern, P. (1995). *An analysis of the model for evaluating HRD programs for the book: Forecasting financial benefits of human resource development.* St. Paul: University of Minnesota, Human Resource Development Research Center.

Sullivan, R., and Elenburg, M. (1988). Performance testing for technical trainers. *Training and Development Journal, 42*(11), 38–40.

Swanson, R.A. (1992). Demonstrating financial benefits to clients. In H. D. Stolovich and E.J. Keeps (Eds.), *Handbook of human performance technology.* San Francisco: Jossey-Bass.

Swanson, R.A. (1989). Everything important in business is evaluated. In R. Brinkerhoff (Ed.), *New directions in program evaluation: Evaluating training programs in business and industry.* San Francisco: Jossey-Bass.

Swanson, R.A., and Gradous, D.B. (1988). *Forecasting financial benefits of human resource development.* San Francisco: Jossey-Bass.

Swanson, R.A., and Mattson, B.W. (1997). Development and validation of the critical outcome technique. In R. Torraco (Ed.), *Academy of Human Resource Development 1996 annual proceedings,* 64–71.

Swanson, R.A., and Sawzin, S.A. (1975). *Industrial training research project.* Bowling Green, OH: Bowling Green State University.

Swanson, R.A., and Sleezer, C.M. (1989). Determining financial benefits of an organization development program. *Performance Improvement Quarterly, 2*(1), 55–65.

Swanson, R.A., and Sleezer, C.M. (1988). Organizational development: What's it worth? *Organizational Development Journal, 6*(1), 37–42.

Tannenbaum, S. (1991). Meeting trainees' expectations: The influence of training fulfillment on the development of commitment, self-efficacy, and motivation. *Journal of Applied Psychology, 76*(6), 759–769.

Tannenbaum, S., and Woods, S. (1992). Determining a strategy for evaluating training: Operating within organizational constraints. *Human Resource Planning, 15*(2), 63–81.

Tessmer, M. (1994). Formative evaluation alternatives. *Performance Improvement Quarterly, 7*(1), 3–18.

Thiagarajan, S. (1991). Formative evaluation in performance technology. *Performance Improvement Quarterly, 4*(2), 22–34.

Thomas, B., Moxham, J., and Jones, J.G.G. (1969). A cost benefit analysis of industrial training. *British Journal of Industrial Relations, 2*(2), 231–264.

Tracey, W. (1981). *Human resource development standards: A self-evaluation manual for HRD managers and specialists.* New York: AMACOM.

Wagner, E. (Ed.). (1993). Variables affecting distance educational program success. *Educational Technology, 33*(4), 28–32.

Wallace, G. (1991). Costing out a training project. *Technical & Skills Training, 2*(4), 29–33.

Wreathall, J., and Connelly, E. (1992). Using performance indicators to evaluate training effectiveness: Lessons learned. *Performance Improvement Quarterly, 5*(3), 35–43.

Zielinski, D. (1991). ROI model gives training new respected cost justification. *Training Directors Forum Newsletter, 7*(6), 4–5.

ABOUT THE AUTHOR

William J. Rothwell is professor of human resource development in the Department of Adult Education, Instructional Systems, and Workforce Education and Development in the College of Education on the University Park Campus of the Pennsylvania State University and director of Penn State's Institute for Research in Training and Development. He also is president of Rothwell and Associates, a private consulting firm with more than 30 multinational corporations on its client list.

Previously, Rothwell was assistant vice president and director of management development for the Franklin Life Insurance Company, Springfield, Illinois, and training director for the Illinois Office of Auditor General. He holds a Ph.D. from the University of Illinois at Urbana-Champaign and has worked full-time in human resource management and employee training and development since 1979, combining real-world experience with academic and consulting experience.

Rothwell's latest publications include *Building In-house Leadership and Management Development Programs* (with H. Kazanas, 2000); *The Competency Toolkit* (with D. Dubois, 2000); *ASTD Models for Workplace Learning and Performance* (with Ethan Sanders and Jeffrey Soper, 1999); *The Action Learning Guidebook* (with K. Sensenig, as editors, 1999); *Sourcebook for Self-Directed Learning* (as editor, 1999); *Creating, Measuring and Documenting Service Impact: A Capacity Building Resource: Rationales, Models, Activities, Methods, Techniques, Instruments* (1998); *In Action: Improving Human Performance* (with D. Dubois, as editors, 1998); *Strategic Human Resource Leader: How to Help Your Organization Manage the Six Trends Affecting the Workforce* (with Prescott and Taylor, as editors, 1998); *In Action: Linking HRD and Organizational Strategy* (as editor, 1998); and *Mastering the Instructional Design Process: A Systematic Approach* (with H. Kazanas, 2nd edition, 1998).

Letters can be addressed to the author at 305C Keller Building, University Park, PA 16803. He can be reached via email at wjr9@psu.edu.

Printed in the United States
204900BV00001B/199-248/A

9 781562 861391